Do your students come to school excited about mathematics? Is math their favorite subject? This program will help you make a difference!

Math

in

Motion

Origami in the Classroom

A Hands-On Creative Approach to Teaching Mathematics

Barbara Elizabeth Pearl, M.A.

ISBN-10: 0-9647924-3-5
ISBN-13: 978-0-9647924-3-2
Copyright ©2008 by Barbara Pearl
All Rights Reserved

In Appreciation. . .

Every book is the work of many hands and I gratefully appreciate and acknowledge the following family and friends:

Jason Seth Houten, my beloved son for his creative spirit, imagination, and illustrations.
Verne Smith, Esq., my loving husband and soulmate for his limitless support and inspiration.
Helene Selig, my mother for her joie de vivre.
Cathy Janson, M.A., my sister for her sense of humour and invaluable ideas.
Carol LeKashman, M.A., architect and friend for reviewing the manuscript.
Maura McDonald, M.F.C.C., school counselor for her editorial comments.
Dr. Patricia Pena-Santana, Gifu University, Japan for all her editorial contributions with the English and Spanish editions of Math in Motion.
Marylyn Rosenblum and Susan Johnson, Brøderbund Software, Inc. for graphics.
Newport Beach Public Library and Staff, for their assistance with research.
Teachers, Students and Families, whom I have learned so much from throughout the years.
Jian Liu, for his remarkable service, Shandong Aomeiya Printing Co. Ltd., Jinan, Shandong, China.
Special thanks to the following for all their thoughtful contributions:
Kurt Reimer, Louise Platt, Dr. Art DuPré, Artie Aszman, Dr. Phyllis Betz, Dr. Mary Robertson, Jane Weinberg, Gerry Johnson, Dr. Faiga Rubinstein, Jessica Gendreau, Wendy Grohol, Rhonda Rea, Jon Rea, Dr. Gary Sheinfeld, Greta Hale and the **Japan America Society of Greater Philadelphia, Chelsea, Zoë, Seven, Scotty, Dylan, Katherine, Sydney, Kitty-Haiku, Trevor, Chopin, Thomas, Sweetheart, Princess, Gray, Silver, Pokey, Allie, Taz and Sheba** for their canine and feline devotion and loyal vigil. Please adopt or foster a cat/dog today.

Acknowledgments. . .

ClickArt and T/Maker Company for software graphics.
Cooking the Chinese Way, Fortune Cookies, by Ling Yu. ©1982 by Lerner Publications. Used by permission of the Publisher. All rights reserved.
Diagrams by John Jacecko, Quantum Labs, Corona del Mar, California.
Grey, L. and Katz, R. (1984). *Fun Folds: Language Learning through Paper Folding.* Tucson, Arizona: Communication Skill Builders.
Graphics reproduced using The Print Shop®; ©1985, 1984, Brøderbund Software, Inc. Used by permission of the Publisher. All rights reserved.
Math Anxiety Cartoon and Japanese Fan by Lindsey and John Minko.
Soloman, D. (1992). Face Folding. Discovery. *New York Newsday.*
Origami made Easy. The Power of Association, p. 15, by Kunihiko Kasahara. ©1973. Japan Publications, Inc. Used by permission of the publisher. All rights reserved.
Origami Models. p. 62, Used by permission. Fox by Mark Leonard, Horse by T. J. Fu.
Origami USA. Jan Polish, Board of Directors. *Teaching Techniques.*
Photograph on page 5 by Margaret Ober, Princeton, New Jersey.
Photographs on pages 9 and 15 by Patricia G. Peña Santana.
Ramney, S. (1993, September). Love Notes. *Arithmetic Teacher*, p. 87.
The Magic of Origami. How to make an Origami Mobile, p. 79, Alice Gray and Kunihiko Kasahara ©1977, Japan Publication Inc., Used by permission of the Publisher. All rights reserved.
The models in this book are 'traditional,' meaning the name of its creator has been lost in history.
If you have additional information about the models, please let us know so that we may credit it.
Math in Motion supports an ecologically sustainable society with the least possible impact on the environment. We are committed to doing this not just through education, but through action.
To help end global deforestation, this book is printed on recycled paper using low VOC inks.
A percentage of sales is donated to humanitarian organizations that support global education.

To Parents and Educators:

*"I think, at a child's birth, if a mother could ask a fairy godmother
to endow it with the most useful gift, that gift should be curiosity."*
— **Eleanor Roosevelt** (1983)

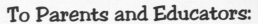

This is not a book on teaching your child *how* to do math. Instead, it is a book on teaching your child to *want* to learn math. Jaime Escalante, a Bolivian immigrant and math teacher portrayed in the film *Stand and Deliver,* turned an impoverished, predominantly Hispanic, East Los Angeles High School into a national math powerhouse. Escalante believed *ganas* (desire) is one of the most important ingredients for learning. How does one begin to instill in children the desire to learn?

One of the primary learning methods for children is imitation. Children often imitate what they hear and see. In the classroom children may hear and see negative messages about mathematics. They associate it with worksheets, textbooks, and tests. Many parents and teachers report they are uncomfortable teaching mathematics and may subconsciously transfer negative messages that influence their children's attitude towards mathematics.

As a national speaker, I meet hundreds of people every year who exclaim, "I hate math! I was never good at math! Math was my worse subject!" These messages perpetuate the cycle that math exclusively focuses on mind-numbing routines and mechanical and technical procedures. I believe that math ability has as much to do with *attitude* as it does with *aptitude*. Here is an approach that will enable all children, no matter what gender or background to succeed in mathematics.

Parent involvement leads to children's success and is one of the ways we can influence our children's development. I began reading aloud and playing math related games with my son, Jason, from an early age, singing nursery rhymes and counting the stars in the galaxy. We collected magnets that framed our refrigerator door and we categorized, sorted, and classified them into people, fruits and letters. At the supermarket, we weighed apples and estimated the price of potatoes. As Jason grew older, he developed a love for reading and mathematics. Once a week we biked to our local library, checked out our favorite books and attended special programs. One day, Michael Shall, The President of Origami USA was teaching an origami workshop at a New York City library. "Hands in lap before you start,"…we were captivated by the beauty, symmetry, and mystery of paper folding.

Math in Motion invites you to discover the creative language of mathematics through *Origami in the Classroom*. I promise you that once you share some of these activities together, they will become one of the best parts of your day and you will treasure them for years to come. So whether you are a student or experienced teacher, an engineer, or a mother raising a family, I hope that you will find some useful ideas in this book and unfold the joys and challenges of learning mathematics.

~*Barbara Elizabeth Pearl*

 # BULLETIN

 **O**hayo (greetings) and welcome. . .to an exciting educational program *where every child counts! Math in Motion* is an interdisciplinary and creative approach to teaching mathematics using origami, the art of paper folding.

 **R**each inside to find a variety of materials for every grade level that will empower you and your students mathematically! One of the greatest Values of *Math in Motion* is a sense of accomplishment and achievement your students will experience as they gain a positive attitude towards math.

 **I**ntegrate these activities into your lesson plans and make math come alive! *Math in Motion* is based on the principle that children *learn by doing* and supports the national goals for "hands-on" active learning.

 **G**eometry, shapes, number sense, patterns, fractions, measurement, problem solving, listening and following directions, and critical and analytical thinking are just some of the valuable skills used to develop meaning and understanding through *Math in Motion.*

 A**LL** children are captivated by the origami experience. *Math in Motion* is committed to demystifying the fear and elitism often associated with mathematics and invites children to feel, touch and see the concepts as they are being taught. Children exclaim, "I did it! I didn't know math could be this much fun! Teach us more!"

 **M**ath in Motion promotes global education, an awareness and appreciation of other cultures. Discover how to blend multi-cultural activities into your lesson plans from haiku to tangrams. Learn to recycle materials including magazines, calendars and maps!

 If you would like to help your child excel in mathematics and discover easy, practical ideas that make learning mathematics FUN--enter the fold with MATH IN MOTION!

Make it Happen in Your Classroom

- Strategies for Getting Students Excited about Mathematics and Learning
- Stimulating Projects to Make your Math Program Soar
- Methods for Boosting your Students' Confidence
- Eliminate Fears of Failure

Building Math Literacy

- Learn to Communicate Mathematically
- Visualizing Math Concepts: Seeing is Believing
- Non-threatening Ways to get Kids to Participate
- Develop a Positive Math Environment for ALL Students

Skill Building without Paper and Pencil

- Organize your Classroom for Active Participation
- Less Disruptive and more On-Task Behavior
- Cooperative Learning Activities to Connect Mathematics
- Across the Curriculum

Teaching for Understanding

- Meaningful "Hands-On" Manipulatives for Developing
- Understanding and Spatial Sense
- Minds in Motion: Learning by Doing
- Proven, Practical, Easy Ideas to Integrate Curriculum Standards
- Promote Diversity through Multicultural Awareness and Activities

In her *Math in Motion* workshop and book, Barbara Pearl has created a wonderfully delightful and practical guide to using origami that makes mathematics come alive in the hands and minds of all children.

Dr. Steven Leinwand, President, National Council of Supervisors of Mathematics (NCSM)

Many of my student teachers hate math and are scared of it. After one of them used *Math in Motion* to demonstrate a lesson, the class broke into spontaneous applause! Your method gave her the confidence to excel. I am convinced that your method is an invaluable tool for all grade levels.

Dr. Davida Fischman, Professor, Mathematics, California State San Bernardino

It was great! Lots of ideas and enthusiasm. Thanks for making our Staff Development Day so successful.

Sandra E. Barry, Assistant Superintendent, Buena Park School District, Buena Park, CA

Barbara is unparalleled in her ability to connect origami to math concepts and spatial skills. I use *Math in Motion* with preservice and inservice teachers as well as children. They now respond to math with great anticipation and joy!

Dr. Janet G. Melancon, Ed.D., Professor, Director of Graduate Education Studies, Loyola University New Orleans

Now millions of viewers have an opportunity to learn about this exciting and innovative method of teaching. I wish I had learned math this way when I was in school!

Gary Collins, Home Show, ABC Television

Math in Motion was a hit! Highly motivating and inspirational. Count us in. Let's do it again.

Kathy Levenshus, PTA President, Family Math Night, Christ Lutheran School, Costa Mesa, CA

Excellent work with student assemblies, great crowd control-children were really excited! Math was everywhere!

David Washington, Kindergarten, New Jersey

Fascinating and dynamic presentation-the children were so attentive and responsive. Next year begins a new approach to math using manipulatives. *Math in Motion* will be a great addition! Come back soon!

Carol Allen, Grade 4, Outstanding Teacher of the Year, Moulton Elementary School, Laguna Niguel, CA

Fabulous insights for our program. *Math in Motion* makes our class come alive!

Mary DeFilippo, Literacy Coordinator, Title 1, Leominster Public School, Leominster, MA

I thoroughly enjoyed your workshop. My student's response to your program was overwhelming!!!

Jeffrey Ballam, Gifted Education, Grade 6, Chapel Hill, NC

I teach high school math-Concrete Math, Algebra I, and Geometry. I have included different pieces that you taught at our inservice in Corpus Christi in 1996. The kids love it! I take the concrete and use it with technology too. Thank you for getting me hooked years ago.

Mary Lankford, Sinton High School, Sinton, TX (email, 1/31/07)

Great for relating math to art especially since I work with students who like to touch to learn! The visuals were an excellent way of introducing math vocabulary and concepts, especially for those who don't like math.

Maria Perez, 3ʳᵈ Grade, Bilingual Education, Los Angeles, CA

Siempre ha sido un reto despertar el interés por las matemáticas en algunos de nuestros estudiantes. *Matemáticas en Movimiento* es una herramienta excelente para conseguirlo. Son fáciles de entender, no son amenazantes...y son simplemente muy divertidas.

Sergio Mery, Director de las Escuelas de Verano, Universidad de Millersville, PA

What Children are Saying...

Your teaching is so nice. I like the way you taught us. I wish I could be a teacher like you.

Joseph Walker, 2ⁿᵈ Grade

Our whole class cherishes your teaching. Your classes are really fun! Can we do more of this?

Minh Nguyen, 4ᵗʰ Grade

I usually don't like math, but now I want to learn. I'm glad we have your lessons and someone is here to help me. I just wish you could stay longer.

Nina Halpern, 6ᵗʰ Grade

All three of my children loved your workshop. After they did every origami activity in your book, they talked about nothing else but you and origami for the six hour ride home!

Peggy Campbell-Rush, Teacher/Author, *I Teach Kindergarten! Staff Development for Educators Conference (SDE)*, Taylor, age 9, Morgan, 12, Mackenzie, 14, Washington, NJ

Aline Esqueda, Humberto López, Stephanie Jiménez and Lumi Kobayashi discover the excitement and joy of mathematics as they unfold a *Math in Motion* origami box.

Table of Contents

*Teacher Scripts

Part VI
Cultural & Educational Enrichment

Part VII
Resources

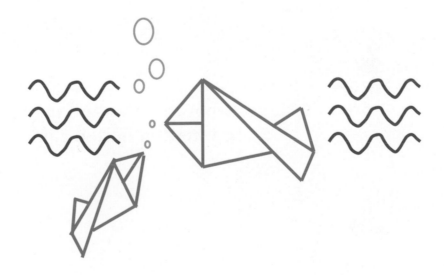

"The journey of a thousand miles
begins with a single step."

...Chinese proverb

"We make a living by what we get,
but we make a life by what we give."

...Winston Churchill

"We have learned so much. I didn't
know math could be this much fun!"

...An eleven year old
girl after a workshop

Visit our website for online support at:
www.mathinmotion.com

Part 1

Introduction
to
Math in Motion

It is the supreme art of the teacher to awaken joy in creative expression and knowledge.

Albert Einstein, Physicist

Introduction

"I hear and I forget. I see and I remember. I do and I understand."

Chinese Proverb

Does your head start to hurt every time you have to solve a math problem? Does your vision get blurry when you try to balance your checkbook? If you feel this way, so do many of my students who suffer from **MATH ANXIETY.** A page of numbers fills them with **PANIC!** In fact, CBS columnist Charles Osgood stated, "Some people have such an aversion to math that when confronted with numbers or calculations their teeth start to ache!"

Math in Motion: Origami in the Classroom draws kids into the world of learning. If you are a teacher or a parent, this book will help you and your kids learn to enjoy and communicate mathematically and discover special methods that focus on student-centered learning to develop your children's math skills. These creative activities are designed to relieve math anxiety, help at-risk students, meet the needs of diverse learners and accommodate a variety of learning styles.

Origami invites children to explore abstract concepts from number sense to geometry. According to the National Council of Teachers of Mathematics, NCTM (1989, 2000), "students need to investigate, explore and manipulate everyday objects to be able to describe relationships in a multi-dimensional world using mathematical language." A hands-on, see-it, say-it, write-it approach brings mathematics to life by linking math to different parts of a curriculum. Susan Sze (2005) states, "Origami stimulates more parts of the brain than the traditional teacher-lecture format… Teachers can apply the knowledge to involve a student in a total learning experience which enhances the student's ability to think critically, to create a class dialogue, and to pose questions to encourage high level of thinking."

By constructing and deconstructing paper manipulatives, building knowledge, and experiencing it first hand, children find learning becomes more meaningful. The shapes and forms kids create with paper folding exercises help them apply math concepts and vocabulary concretely, retain information longer and bridge the gap between words and their meaning.

Math in Motion is a valuable resource that will add an exciting dimension to your math learning environment. Through the paper folding process children feel motivated to learn. This successful program is easy to use and demonstrates proven, practical and non-threatening ways to bring out the best from your most reluctant, "I-HATE-MATH" to gifted students. *Math in Motion* supports national goals, principles, and standards—to help **ALL** children succeed in mathematics!

Lindsey Minko

History of Origami

折紙
ori　gami

What is the history of origami?

Origami, the Japanese name for the art of paper folding, comes from the Japanese verb *oru* (to fold) and the noun *kami* (paper). A finished origami figure is called a *model*, and instructions for a model is called a *diagram*. The origin of paper folding is traced back to over 1000 years ago to parts of Europe and China. Buddhist monks then carried paper from china by way of Korea into Japan. As paper was so precious and expen$ive, it was originally preserved by the religious leaders and emperors. For centuries origami was associated with traditional Japanese ceremonies; but, overtime it became a family pastime and was handed down from one generation to the next.

Who were some famous paper folders?

An origami artist is usually called a paper folder. Some famous paper folders include Leonardo da Vinci (1452-1519), a renaissance painter, architect, engineer, mathematician and philosopher, who explored a number of geometric paper folding exercises in his study on the velocity and motion of paper; Friedrich Fröbel (1782-1852), a German educator who founded the kindergarten system in the 1800's and used origami to familiarize children with geometric shapes; Lewis Carroll (1832-1898), a mathematician and the author of *Alice in Wonderland* who entertained children of royalty with origami; Miguel de Unamuno (1864-1936), a Spanish philosopher and poet; Harry Houdini (1874-1926), a magician and the author of one of the first English origami books published in 1922. Today there are active origami societies throughout the world that link cultures and nations together. Origami attracts people from all over the world and many enthusiasts are mathematicians, scientists and engineers. Peter Engel, an architect, in *Folding the Universe* refers to origami as the "mathematician's art."

Why is origami so special?

Origami is special because all you need is a piece (peace) of paper. Throughout history the crane has been recognized as an international symbol of *peace*. According to Japanese legend if you fold one thousand cranes you will get your wish and live a long life. The legend of the crane is illustrated in Eleanor Coerr's children's story, *Sadako and the Thousand Paper Cranes*. Paper folding also has many therapeutic benefits and is used in speech, mental health, and occupational therapy. After a Math in Motion workshop, Seth, an enthusiastic fifth grader said, "It's just like a journey inside the paper!" My days can be hectic, but with origami I can put *everything* in order." Tomoko Fuse, a celebrated and prolific origami author, relates, "All origami begins with putting the hands into motion. Understanding something intellectually and knowing the same thing tactilely are very different."

For more information on the history of origami, visit: www.paperfolding.com/history.

Mathematics & Origami

AUGUST

"A mathematician, like a painter or poet, is a maker of patterns...with ideas."
Godfrey H. Hardy (1877-1947)

A square is transformed into a box
A square is transformed into a bird
A square is transformed into a snake
A square is transformed into an elephant.

Unless one knew better, one would think we were talking about a magic show or topology[1].

Origami is an art form that dates back to 583 A.D. when Buddhist monks brought paper into Japan from China through Korea. Since the manufacturing of paper at that time was costly, people used it with care, and origami became an integral part of certain ceremonies. The art of origami has been shared and passed on from generation to generation. Animals, flowers, boats, and people have all been created with origami.

an origami swan

(The word origami is derived from *ori-to fold* and *gami-paper*).

Origami has delighted enthusiasts over the centuries. In fact, today there are many international origami societies established in Britain, Belgium, France, Italy, Japan, The Netherlands, New Zealand, Peru, Spain and the United States[2].

In creating an origami figure, the origamist begins with a square sheet of paper and transforms it into any shape limited only by his or her imagination, skill and determination. A square was probably chosen as the original starting unit of origami because it possesses 4

Kumiko Yamaguchi (fifth grade) and Lumi Kobayashi (first grade) explore, investigate and discover the precision, excitement and joy of mathematics as they unfold a *Math in Motion* box.

lines of symmetry, unlike the rectangle or other quadrilaterals. Although some other regular polygons and circles have more lines of symmetry, they lack the right angles of the square, and would have been more difficult to manufacture. Sometimes origamists do begin with other units, but the purists work with squares without using glue or scissors.

A study of the creases impressed on the square sheet of paper, after an origami object has been created, reveals a wealth of geometric objects and properties. This diagram shows the creases that were impressed on a square when it was folded into a flying bird. The creases on a square can illustrate the mathematical ideas of similarities, lines and points of symmetry, congruence, ratio and proportions of shape, and iterations

(continual repetitions of patterns within patterns) resembling the formation of geometric fractals. Studying the progression of an origami creation is very enlightening. One begins with a square (a 2-dimensional object), and then manipulates the square to form a figure (a 3-dimensional object). If it is a new creation, the origamist will unfold the figure and study the creases impressed on the square. This process involves moving between dimensions. The creases represent the object's 2-dimensional projection onto a flat plane, namely the square. A transformation of a 2-D object to a 3-D object and back is related to the field of projective geometry.

In the book *Folding the Universe*, author Peter Engel, a master of the art and science of origami, reveals his years of work, unique discoveries and creations in origami. Engel has taken origami to a

whole new plateau, which emphasizes the strong connection between origami, mathematics, and nature by drawing analogies to minimization problems, fractals and the chaos theory. An origami creation begins with a finite amount of material (e.g. a square of fixed dimensions) and evolves into a desired form, without the restrictions placed upon nature in the formation of natural forms, such as bubbles.

Origami is experiencing a renaissance. It has come a long way from the foundations developed by early paper folders. The complexity of the figures folded by today's masters are truly amazing. Their skill in transforming a square sheet of paper, without the use of scissors or glue, is incredible. The completed forms are not simple boxes or flowers, but anatomically accurate animals, realistic life like paper sculptures, squid, spiders, snakes, dancers, furniture. To achieve such proficiency and creativity takes years of work, experience and study. It is analogous to the years which artists like M.C. Escher devoted to developing the art of tessellations. The mathematics, whether identified as such by origamists, is there. Like tessellation art, the understanding of mathematics enhances one's ability and creativity.

[1]Topology is a special kind of geometry that studies properties of an object that remain unchanged when the object is distorted by being stretched or shrunk. Unlike Euclidean geometry, topology does not deal with size, shape, or rigid figures. This is why topology is often referred to as rubber sheet geometry. Imagine objects existing on rubber sheets that can be stretched and shrunk. In the process of these transformations, one studies the characteristics that remain unchanged.

[2]Origami USA at the American Museum of Natural History, 15 West 77th St., NY, NY 10024. Ph. (212) 769-5635 / www.origami-usa.org.

From: *The Mathematics Calendar 1991* and *More Joy of Mathematics* by Theoni Pappas ©1991. Reprinted by permission of Wide World Publishing/Tetra, San Carlos, CA.

Careers ✏ Choices

Opportunities

$$\infty 5\phi 8x1 \leq 4 \geq 2\%6\#7@\,\$9 \div 3\pi 0 \neq >$$

Many career opportunities are related to mathematics. Not all of these jobs require advanced math skills. Here are some of the rewarding careers that utilize math skills and critical thinking. Choose one of the careers and answer the following questions:

1) What kind of work does this person do?

2) How is math used in that career?

3) What is the income they could earn?

Accountant	Financial Advisor
Actuary	Geologist
Aerospace Engineer	Meteorologist
Airline Pilot	Navigator
Archeologist	Oceanographer
Architect	Optometrist
Astronaut	Physician
Astronomer	Radiologist
Banker	Scientist
Biologist	Seismologist
Computer Analyst	Surveyor
Dentist	Technical Writer
Engineer	U.S. Navy Officer…

Part II
Fundamentals

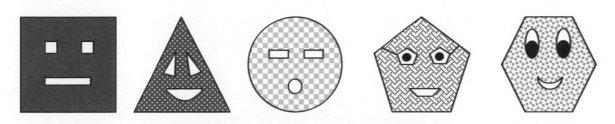

All things are possible until they are proved impossible.
Pearl S. Buck, Author

Math in Motion...Where Every Child Counts!
Educational Benefits of Origami
101 Ways to Use Origami in Your Classroom

In Japan, children learn origami at home and in kindergarten. Today, many schools in the West integrate origami in the classrooms. Research has shown that paper folding, particularly in the elementary school years, is a unique and valuable addition to the curriculum (Sze, 2005). Origami is not only fun, but also an innovative method for developing educational, cultural and social skills.

Mathematics
- Develop Shape, Size and Color Recognition
- Develop Math Concepts and Vocabulary
- Develop Geometric Fundamentals, Measurement
- Symmetry, Congruence, Lines, Angles, Vertices
- Investigate 3-Dimensional Objects/ Spatial Sense
- Develop Fractions, Ratio, Proportion
- Increase Writing in the Mathematics Class
- Develop Problem Solving and Critical Thinking
- Explore Patterns and Make Connections

Language Arts
- Recognize Pictorial Representations & Symbols
- Develop Reading Comprehension/ Verbal and
- Vocabulary Cues/ Interpret and Analyze Diagrams
- Apply Differentiated Instruction/ Multiple Intelligences
- Develop Organizational/ Communication Skills
- Create a Journal log or Word Wall Book
- Stimulate Creative Writing/ Storytelling & Puppets
- Connect Multicultural Children's Literature

Art
- Nurture Creativity and Challenge Imagination
- Explore Original Ideas Using Origami: Mobiles
- Jewelry, Dioramas, Ornaments, Decorations
- Experiment with Different Materials and Textures
- Recycle Gift Wrapping Paper, Magazines, Maps,
- Flyers, Calendars, Newspapers and Posters
- Decorate a Bulletin Board/ Seasonal Displays
- Arrange an Origami Exhibit at your School,
- Local Library or Museum – Contact the Media

Science
- Fold Origami Animals, Birds, Insects, Flowers
- Celebrate Earth Day April 22 - Fold a Whale!
- Go Green - Recycle Paper Resources
- Test if Origami Boats Float/ Cups Hold Water
- Explore the Aerodynamics of Paper Airplanes
- Research Endangered Species – Fold a Frog
- Promote Scientific Inquiry: Observe & Measure
- the Distance of Origami Jumping Frogs—
- Tabulate the Data and Graph the Results

Social Studies
- Increase Multicultural Awareness
- Promote Peace and Humane Education
- Send Cranes to Hiroshima, Japan on Peace Day,
- August 6th (Anniversary of the Bombing)
- Illustrate Holidays (Columbus Day-Sailboats)
- Foster Friendship—Write an Asian Pen Pal
- Explore the Music and History of the East
- Fold a Wolf! Learn to Protect Wildlife

Social Skills
- Develop Listening Skills/ Following Directions
- Develop Pro-Social Skills—Attitude, Patience
- Perseverance, Precision, Cooperation, Respect
- Improve Concentration, Memory and Retention
- Develop Eye-Hand Coordination/ Fine Motor
- Foster Cooperative Learning and Socialization
- Increase Motivation, Confidence & Self Esteem
- Organize a Family Math Night – Promote
- School-Home Connection

References:

"An Analysis of Constructivism and the Ancient Art of Origami," Susan Sze, Niagara University, Innovations in Inclusive School Development, Conference Proceedings, 2005.
"Bringing Constructivity into the Classroom," Walter Enloe and Karen Evans, University of Minnesota, 1993.
The Child's Conception of Space, Jean Piaget and B. Inhelder, Routledge & Kegan Paul, 1956.

Square Power

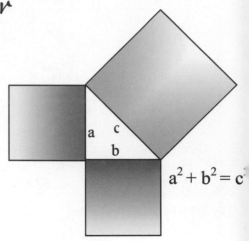

$$a^2 + b^2 = c^2$$

Establish an environment that encourages risk taking; be sure it is a "safe" place to investigate ideas and to try them out. Examine the folds made from a single sheet of square paper. These are simple folds requiring no special creativity or skill; but if you apply your imagination you will be able to see many different shapes and forms.

Roger von Oech, *A Whack on the Side of the Head: How You Can Be More Creative* states, "In the ten year period between kindergarten and high school, not only had we learned how to be specific, but we had lost much of our imaginative power." As noted educator, Neil Postman, remarked, "Children enter schools as question marks and leave as periods."

Invite your students to take a plain square sheet of paper and see how many shapes they can create. What do they see…kites, ice cream cones, diamonds, books, mountains, birds, butterflies or spaceships? Turn the paper in different directions and examine it from different angles. List how many objects you can find.

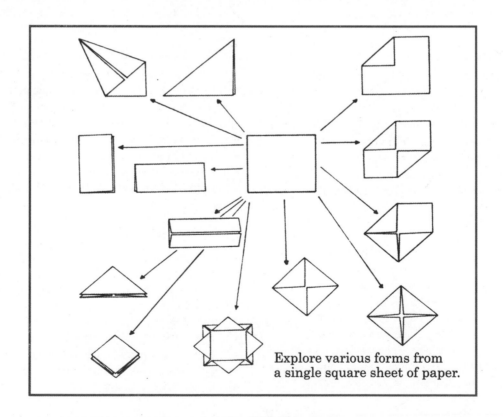

Explore various forms from a single square sheet of paper.

Folding Concepts

Develop mathematics concepts and vocabulary
in context to develop content standards.

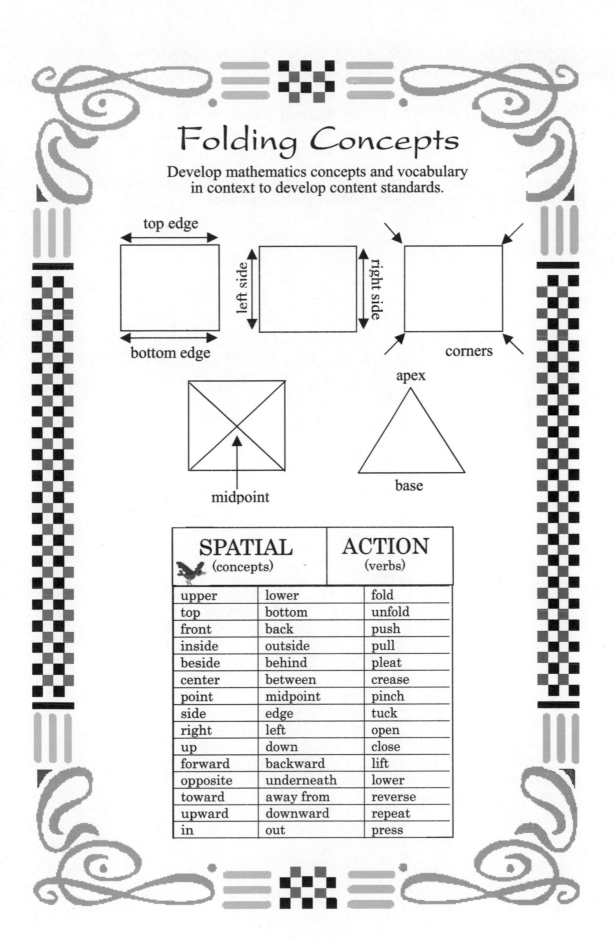

SPATIAL (concepts)		ACTION (verbs)
upper	lower	fold
top	bottom	unfold
front	back	push
inside	outside	pull
beside	behind	pleat
center	between	crease
point	midpoint	pinch
side	edge	tuck
right	left	open
up	down	close
forward	backward	lift
opposite	underneath	lower
toward	away from	reverse
upward	downward	repeat
in	out	press

CELEBRATE GEOMETRY! Study the patterns below. The four fundamental Bases—Kite, Fish, Bird, and Frog are related geometrically. The Kite Base is demonstrated in the *Whale* model (p. 58). The other bases involve more advanced techniques. Fold a model and then *unfold* it. Study, examine, explore, analyze, compare and contrast the geometric patterns. Challenge students to create their own models and patterns. What other models can you create? Color the paper patterns and display in the classroom.

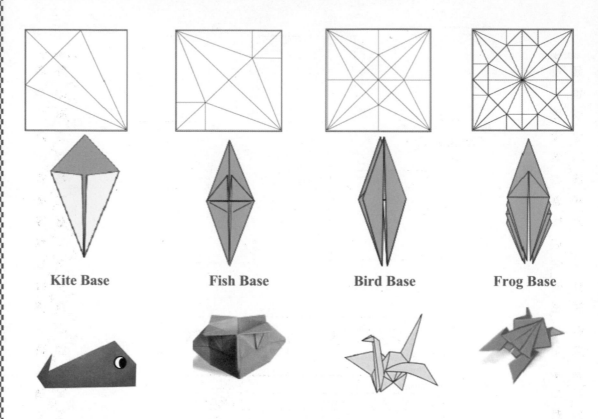

Kite Base   Fish Base   Bird Base   Frog Base

GEOMETRY		QUANTITATIVE	QUALITATIVE
polygon	angle	length	texture
square	vertex	width	smooth
rectangle	hexagon	height	thick
triangle	isosceles	area	thin
octagon	quadrilateral	volume	plain
trapezoid	pentagon	perimeter	pattern

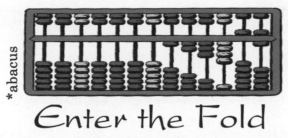

*abacus

Enter the Fold
*Analyzing an Origami Diagram

Materials: Paper • Pencil • Ruler (see *How to Make a Square*, p. 56)
Students can use notebook or copy paper to make squares.

Alternative: Precut Squares. Give each group 4 squares.

Instructions: Copy *Diagram for First Folds* on the chalkboard or an overhead.

Use this exercise to introduce or reinforce shape recognition, mathematics vocabulary and concepts. Students fold and analyze each square pattern. (Younger students can copy the square patterns on their paper squares and trace the shapes). There are *many* responses for the squares below. List observations on the squares or discuss responses and write them on the board.

✐*Note to Teacher: Analyzing an origami diagram encourages problem solving and critical thinking skills. Delight in your children's thinking, ask: "What can we say about the shape? Does anyone have a different idea? Why do you think that?" Students discover there can be more than one right answer and more than one way of looking at any problem or situation.

Diagram for First Folds
Book Fold is an origami term used when a square or rectangle is folded in half. It resembles a book.

Book Fold   **Two Book Folds**

Diagonal Fold   **Two Diagonal Folds**

1. The square is divided into 2 rectangles.
2. The vertical line is a line of symmetry.
3. The lines are parallel.

1. The square is divided into 4 squares.
2. There are 5 squares all together.
3. The lines form perpendicular lines.

1. The square is divided into 2 triangles.
2. The triangles are the same size (congruent).
3. The triangles are isosceles right triangles.

1. The square is divided into 4 triangles.
2. Each triangle is ¼ of the square.
3. The lines form perpendicular lines.

 *An **abacus** is a calculation tool, often constructed as a wooden frame with beads sliding on wires. It was in use centuries before the adoption of the written Hindu-Arabic numeral system and is still widely used by merchants and clerks in China, Japan, Hong Kong, Africa and elsewhere.

Challenge Page...The Next Fold

**Here are more challenging folds to explore. Try folding the square patterns.
List three responses or more for each square and compare your observations.**

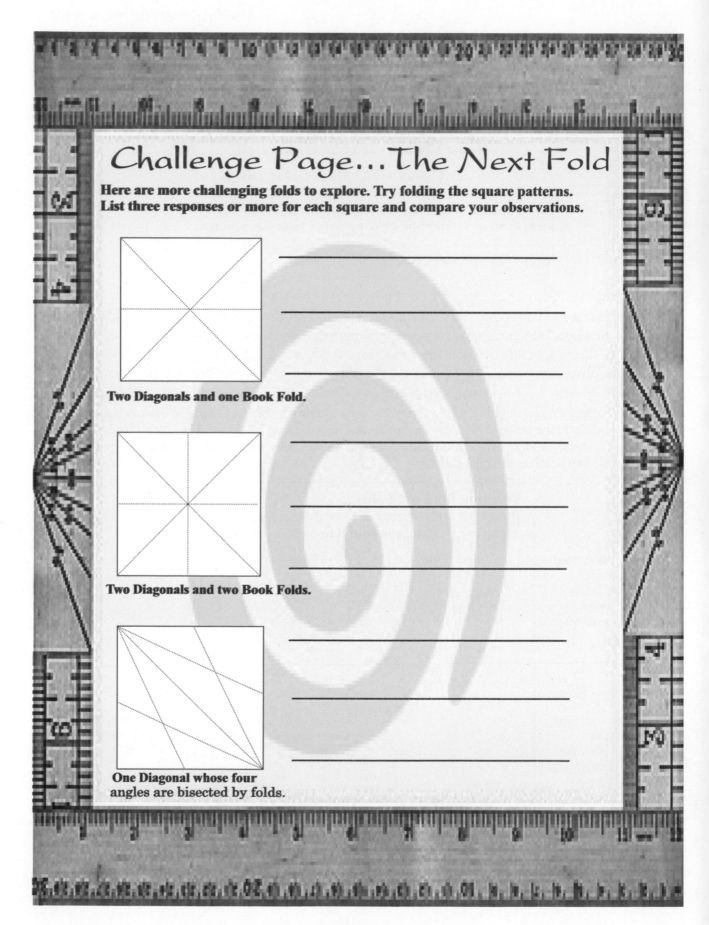

Two Diagonals and one Book Fold.

_____

_____

_____

Two Diagonals and two Book Folds.

_____

_____

_____

**One Diagonal whose four
angles are bisected by folds.**

_____

_____

_____

Part III

Techniques

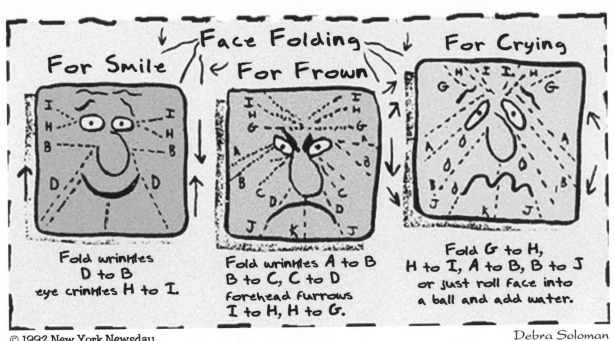

For Smile

Face Folding

For Frown

For Crying

Fold wrinkles
D to B
eye crinkles H to I.

Fold wrinkles A to B
B to C, C to D
forehead furrows
I to H, H to G.

Fold G to H,
H to I, A to B, B to J
or just roll face into
a ball and add water.

Debra Soloman

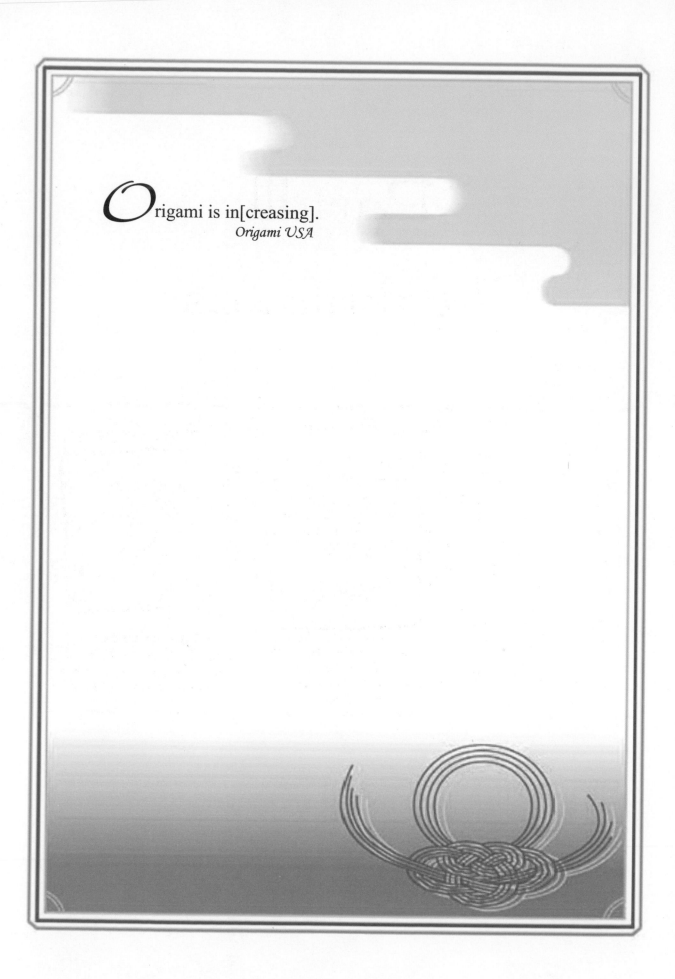

*O*rigami is in[creasing].
Origami USA

Principles of Paper Folding

Excellence is not an act but a habit. The things you do the most are the things you will do best. –Marva Collins

*Prior to teaching, review the characteristics that develop successful learning habits. Add other attributes for building Character Education: attitude, respect, responsibility, cooperation, consideration, perseverance.

PATIENCE

Patience means the willingness to
take the time to learn a new skill
(to listen carefully and to
follow directions).
The more patient you are
the better your results will be.

 ## PRECISION

Precision means to be exact and careful.
The more precise you fold the
nicer your model will look.

PRACTICE

Practice makes progress.
The more you practice the
more progress you will make.

*See Habits of Mind: www.habitsofmind.org

 Kimonos were the traditional clothing of Japan. They were worn by women, men and children. There are styles of kimonos for various occasions, ranging from extremely formal to very casual. Today kimonos are used for special occasions and holidays.

PAPER RESOURCES

T raditional origami paper is precut into squares ranging in size, color and pattern. It is usually color on one side and white on the other side. The 6-8 inch paper square is easier to manipulate and good for beginners. Origami paper is available in most craft stores, online or from Math in Motion (see Order Form, pp 119-120).

R eading, writing and arithmetic are the 3Rs we want our children to master academically. Zoe Weil, Co-founder and President of the Institute for Humane Education states, "Reverence, Respect and Responsibility are the 3Rs we want our children to master socially." Character counts-teach children to put compassion into action and protect the environment.

E ncourage students to recycle: magazines, calendars, gift wrap, greeting cards, postcards, book covers, flyers and post-it-notes. Ask parents to recycle items from their home and office. Start a recycling resource box in your classroom; visit travel agencies for brochures, garage sales for maps and video stores for promotional posters. Trim to size with a paper cutter.

E xperiment with a variety of papers. Use practice papers until you are familiar with the model and then have fun choosing a pattern that will enhance your project. Students can draw their own designs, create them on a computer or use graphics, clip art and coloring pages from the Internet (see sample patterns, pp. 29-30).

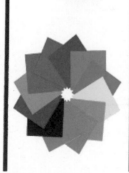

SAV-A-TREE

by G. E. Om-etry

RECYCLE, REDUCE, RE-USE

Have fun experimenting with different patterns, prints and clip art on the Internet to personalize and enhance your projects.

29

Color Your World

Monarch Butterflies Color the page and then fold into a box and display, see p. 47.
Many classrooms study the migration of the monarch butterflies. Every year, when the weather turns
cooler, millions of monarch butterflies travel hundreds of miles to spend the winter in warmer places.
In the spring they return, laying eggs along the way. The eggs develop into caterpillars that spin cocoons
and then emerge as adult butterflies. Source: Check out the National Geographic video and more coloring
pages at: www.nationalgeographic.com/coloringbook/butterflies.html. For primary grades, see:
http://www.first-school.ws/ or http://free-coloring-pages.com/.

Ten
Teaching Techniques

FUN FACTS: Alliteration is the matching or repetition of consonants or the repeating of the same letter (or sound) at the beginning of words following each other immediately or at short intervals. For Example: Ten Teaching Techniques (each word starts with the same letter, T). Principles of Paper folding (short intervals), or the famous tongue twister, "Peter Piper picked a peck of pickled peppers." Alliteration is often found in poetry. Create your own examples.

1. Begin with a simple model. Place yourself where all the students can see your hands and the sample. If not everyone can see you at once, repeat the step for each side of the room. Encourage students to *observe* your demonstration of each step before they attempt it.

2. Choose larger paper to demonstrate. Your sample should be large enough to be seen from the back row, but not too large to manipulate. Precrease your model so that you can pay attention to your class. Highlight the lines on *your* model using different color markers or crayons to identify the folds so that everyone can see the next step.

3. Fold on a firm surface like a table or a book. Emphasize folding neatly and accurately. Crease each step sharply at least *three* times. The sharper you fold, the easier it will be to see and follow the creases and guidelines.

4. Try to ensure that your students are quiet and attentive. Students must be able to listen and follow directions in a *supportive* learning environment. See *Habits of Mind* to develop essential and lifelong learning skills at: www.habitsofmind.org.

5. Encourage students to explore the qualitative and quantitative characteristics of the materials and shapes they use. Ask: "How does this paper feel? What color is it? What can we say about the shape we see?" This open-ended question approach encourages students to analyze the figure without the pressure of obtaining one right answer. It also enables the teacher to assess what the class already knows and what they may need to learn.

6. While teaching each step to the class, introduce math concepts and vocabulary (see *Concepts and Vocabulary* for each model) so that your students can experience them first hand and learn them in context. Have students identify and label each part of the model on their paper. Younger children can trace the areas with their fingers as they recite the parts of the figure.

7. When describing a fold, try to avoid saying, "fold like this or that." Give "landmarks" or other cues and mention the place where the fold begins and ends. Orient your sample the same way your students are folding. Treat each step as one unit: first identify the present position and orientation of the model, perform the step, and then confirm the new position. Make sure each of your students has performed this step correctly. If you sense any uncertainty, repeat your instructions. Try to find a clearer explanation. If a step is challenging, ask students to hold their papers up to check the whole class at the same time or *encourage* them to help each other.

8. Avoid folding the student's model. Frustration and failure may alienate them from trying. Establish that a raised hand signals a sign for help without disturbing others. Help individual students or assign another student to assist them. If you have to perform the step on their model, unfold it and let them try it again. *Self-satisfaction* is very important. If they are still unable to perform the step, you may need to fold their model to enable them to complete it. With practice, they will quickly (tout de suite) develop the confidence they need to succeed.

9. Be supportive and nonthreatening in your instructions and corrections. Everyone learns at a different pace. Some students may seem more cautious than others and may be afraid to fail and make mistakes. Give the class as much reassurance and *positive* encouragement as possible. If you enjoy teaching and learning with origami, your students will too! Remember to also be patient with yourself, take your time and most of all…

10. **Have Fun!**

May the fold be with you!

Part IV
Teaching Guidelines

(Please Review before Teaching)

That's the way things come clear. All of a sudden.
And then you realize how obvious they've been all along.
Madeleine L'Engle, Author, The Arm of the Starfish

Lesson Plan Guide

The math-oriented curriculum was developed to provide the classroom teacher or specialist with a general framework to support National Standards and curriculum requirements. Many of the activities were chosen to provide specific development of the elementary students' auditory, verbal, visual and motor growth. Four (4) of the models (*Box, *Frog, *Whale, and *Dog) in *How to Fold*...demonstrate questions formulated specifically for the mathematics class. See *Teacher Scripts in the *Table of Contents*. The professional is encouraged to adapt and modify these activities according to their students' capabilities.

Objectives:

- **To develop auditory and visual attention skills** (listening and following directions)

- **To develop visual-motor skills** (eye-hand coordination)

- **To develop temporal-spatial concepts** (the ability to understand the position of self and objects in relation to each other)

- **To develop shape, size, color and pattern recognition** (exploring, investigating, making connections, identifying, creating, communicating)

- **To develop sequencing skills** (retain and recall information in appropriate order)

- **To develop basic geometric principles** (concrete models, constructing and deconstructing, relationships, patterns, vocabulary and concepts)

- **To integrate mathematics with other subjects** (Language Arts, Social Studies, Music, Art, Drama, Multicultural Education and Technology)

- **To develop an awareness and appreciation for cultural diversity** (respect, tolerance and compassion for others)

IMPORTANT

PROCEDURE

 guide is provided for folding the models in this book: 1) Review *Ten Teaching Techniques* pp. 31-32. Study Parts II - IV. 2) As you become more familiar with teaching each model, refer to these sections when necessary to extend the lesson.

PROJECTS:
The projects are divided into three geometric shapes: rectangles, squares and triangles. They range in complexity from simple to intermediate and are presented in that order, although there is some variation within each group.

RECYCLE:
Students can use their notebook paper, flyers, posters, and other materials (require one side blank for writing or drawing). Some of the teaching activities and exercises can be transferred to an overhead or chalkboard.

TEACH:
Activate prior knowledge. Model the process step-by-step. At each step introduce or review the *Concepts and Vocabulary* for each project. During the lesson encourage divergent thinking. Ask: "What can we say about the shape?" Divergent thinking challenges students to consider all the possibilities. This open-ended question approach encourages students to analyze the figure without the pressure of obtaining one right answer. It enables the teacher to assess what the class already knows and find out more about *how* they think.

WRITE:
Ask students to write the vocabulary word on the part of the paper that represents that place. *Having the information go in your ears and out of your hands helps you learn it.* Discuss its definition. Activate prior knowledge. Look for other examples in the room to make connections. For younger children, write the word on the board as they say it out loud and trace the place on the paper with their fingers. When students get to feel, touch and see the concepts being taught, it reinforces learning and enhances retention and memory.

ABCDEFGHIJKLMNOPQRSTUVWXYZ

Helpful Hints: Emphasize the rules—

1. Fold precisely (neatly and accurately).
2. Crease each step sharply (at least 3x).

REMEMBER:
Every fold is a <u>guideline.</u> It will guide you to the next place on the paper. Diagrams communicate the progression of the fold as well as verbal instructions. Each drawing shows two things: 1) *the result of the previous step,* and 2) *what action is next.* Before folding the next step shown, l👁👁k ahead to see the results. Emphasize the rules--the more *precise* you fold, the nicer the model will look. The *sharper* you crease, the easier it will be to see the guidelines.

Cross ~ Reference Chart

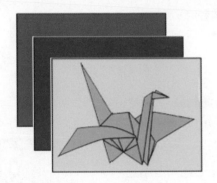

Math in Motion

	Mathematics	Language Arts	Reading	Social Studies	Science	Animals	Water	Holidays	Seasons	Transportation
Box	✓	✓	✓					✓		
Candy Cane	✓	✓	✓					✓		
Cat	✓	✓	✓		✓	✓		✓		
Cup	✓	✓	✓		✓		✓	✓		
Dog	✓	✓	✓		✓	✓				
Fish	✓	✓	✓		✓	✓	✓			
Heart	✓	✓	✓					✓		
Journal	✓	✓	✓	✓	✓					
Jumping frog	✓	✓	✓		✓	✓	✓			
Picture frame	✓	✓	✓					✓		
Pig	✓	✓	✓		✓	✓				
Sailboat	✓	✓	✓	✓	✓		✓	✓		✓
Sailor's Hat	✓	✓	✓	✓						
Tulip	✓	✓	✓		✓		✓	✓	✓	
Whale	✓	✓	✓		✓	✓	✓			
Wolf	✓	✓	✓		✓	✓				

Origami isn't Just for Squares

Math in Motion uses three basic geometric  shapes in paper folding projects -- rectangles, squares and triangles.

Models made from Rectangles...the shape of this page can also be made from student notebook or copy paper. There are many sources of rectangular shapes to recycle. See *Paper Resources*, p. 28.

Models made from Squares... are the most traditional shape used for origami. Use a paper cutter to trim the paper precisely into a square from a rectangle. See *How to Make a Square from a Rectangle*, p. 56.

Models made from Triangles... often start with an isosceles right triangle. Isosceles triangles have two sides the same length. Right triangles have one square corner. Isosceles right triangles have both. See *How to Make an Isosceles Right Triangle*, p. 72.

Part V
Paper Folding
Projects

If you can dream it, you can make it so.
Belva Davis, Journalist

Symbols

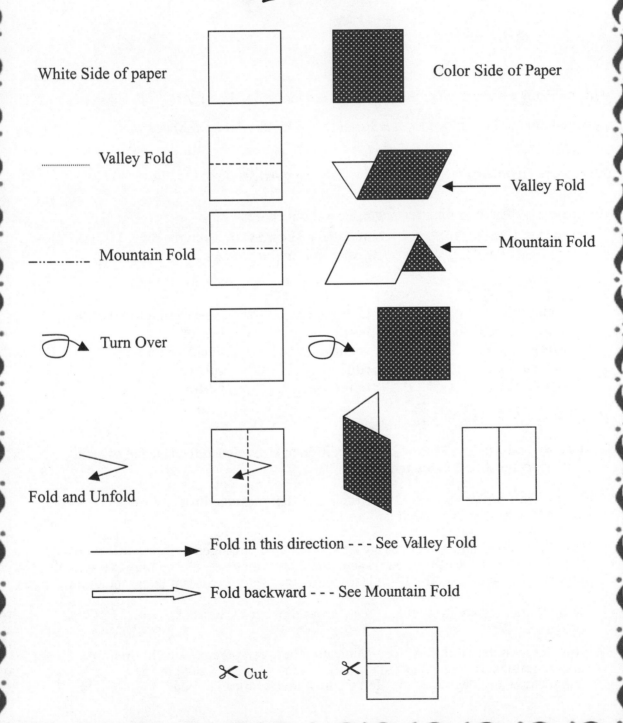

White Side of paper

Color Side of Paper

·········· Valley Fold

Valley Fold

-·-·-·- Mountain Fold

Mountain Fold

Turn Over

Fold and Unfold

Fold in this direction - - - See Valley Fold

Fold backward - - - See Mountain Fold

✂ Cut

Models Made from Rectangles

This model is easy. Practice random acts of kindness. Send ✉ hearts ♥ to a sister school, nursing home or Peace Pal 👧 (see Resources, *The Global Link Newsletter*).

Strand: Geometry ● Spatial Sense ● Language Arts ● Social Studies

Materials: A red or pink rectangle, 8.5 x 2.5 inch
Alternative: Use the strip left over after you make a square from the 8.5 x 11 inch rectangle. See *How to Make a Square from a Rectangle,* p. 56.

Concepts and Vocabulary:

rectangle	pentagon	isosceles right triangle
apex	base	length
width	vertical	line of symmetry
congruent	edge	corner
right/left	top	bottom

Additional Activities:

1 Make several Math in Motion hearts of different sizes. Teach the concept of small, smaller, smallest or big, bigger, biggest.

2 Make a heart for Valentine's Day. Write a heartfelt message inside. Write a poem of love and friendship and attach it to the heart.

3 Make up an anagram. Anagrams are letters that are rearranged to form other words or phrases like heart = earth, listen = silent, the eyes = they see, eleven plus two = twelve plus one. Can you find others? To learn more, visit: http://wordsmith.org/anagram.

4 For St. Patrick's Day make three green hearts to form a shamrock. ☘

5 Write LOVE notes. Reinforce communication between parents and children. Make it a ritual. Tape the heart to the child's shirt with a message inside. "Ask me how my day went" or "Tell me how much I mean to you."

Heart

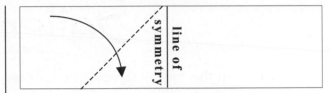

1 Start with a rectangle, white side up. Place on the table with the length (long edges) at the top and bottom. Fold in half widthwise (Book Fold). Unfold.

2 Fold the top left edge down along the line of symmetry (center crease).

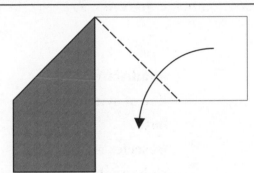

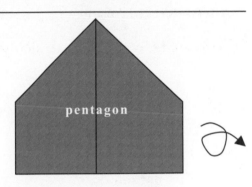

3 Fold the top right edge down to meet the center crease.

4 It looks like a tent. Turn over.

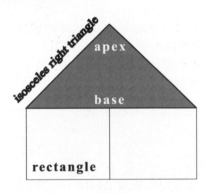

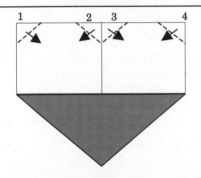

5 Now it looks like a house.

6 Turn the top around to the bottom. See the four corners at the top. Fold each corner down to form a small triangle.

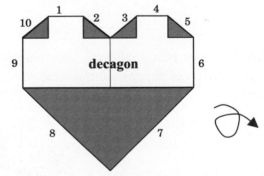

7 Now it looks like this. Count the ten (10) sides--you have a decagon! Turn over.

8 Write a special message inside. Make up a heartfelt saying. I love MATH! Teaching is a work of heart! I ♥ you!

43

Sailor's Hat

You can wear this model. Have a parade or fashion show.

Strand: Geometry • Spatial Sense • Language Arts

Materials: 8.5 x 11 inch rectangle (notebook or copy paper, recycle color flyers)
  Alternative: Make a newspaper hat you can wear (see *Additional Activities, #1*).

Concepts and Vocabulary:

rectangle	side	quadrilateral
right	left	line of symmetry
vertical line	apex	base
pentagon	triangle	isosceles right triangle
bottom	edge	right angle

Additional Activities:

1. Make the sailor's hat out of newspaper to fit your head. Use a standard single sheet of newspaper approximately 22 x 13 inch. Ask parents and neighbors to save the Sunday comics for a colorful hat. Hint: Newspaper is springy, crease sharply!

2. Be creative. Decorate a hat. Provide a wide range of materials. Glue on sequins, beads, felt, ribbon, lace, velvet, pipe cleaners, noodles.

3. Write your name, school or team on the front rim of the hat and "I ♥ Math" on the back.

4. Turn the hat upside down, punch holes on the sides and staple yarn or string as a strap for a one-of-a-kind shoulder bag.

5. Read *Curious George Rides a Bike* by H. A. Rey. Discover how to recycle your hat into a boat (instructions included). Make the boat out of different paper materials and test how long each boat can stay afloat! Graph the results.

Sailor's Hat

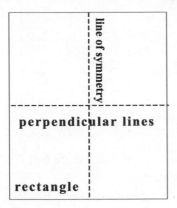

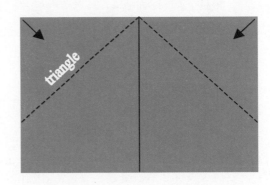

1 Start with an 8.5 x 11 inch rectangle or a sheet of newspaper approximately 22 x 13 inches. Fold in half lengthwise. Unfold. Now, fold in half widthwise.

2 Fold outer corners along diagonal dotted lines to meet at the centerline.

Fold this step if using 8.5" x 11" paper

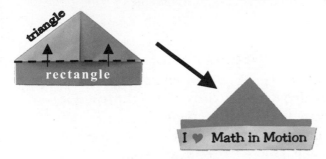

3a Fold TOP LAYER OF PAPER ONLY, along the bottom edge of the horizontal dotted line over triangles. Repeat on the other side. Your paper hat is finished!

Fold steps 3b-5 to make a newspaper hat you can wear.

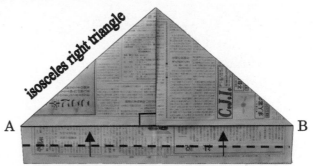

3b Fold TOP LAYER OF PAPER ONLY, along the bottom edge of the horizontal dotted line up to line **AB** (see arrows).

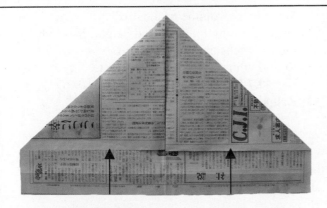

4 Fold the bottom edge up again over the triangles to lock in place. Turn the hat over and repeat steps 3 and 4 on the other side.

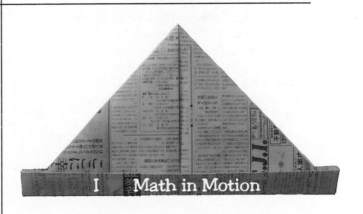

5 Aye, aye, Captain! Your newspaper hat is ready to wear.

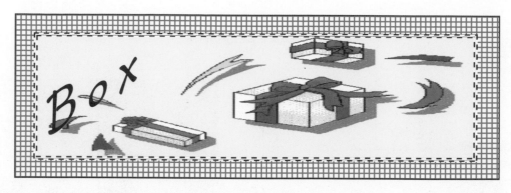

This model was traditionally known as the "magazine box" because it was made out of magazine covers. Make two the same size and connect them together.

FUN FACTS: Paul Weinberg, a grandfather had an exhibit of his origami boxes made out of magazine covers at a New York library. He called the display, "Literary Origami."

Strand: Fractions • Geometry • Art

Materials: 8.5 x 11 inch rectangle (color copy paper)

Alternative: For a decorative box, recycle the front and back covers of magazines.

Concepts and Vocabulary:

Fractions		Geometry	
whole	1	rectangle	perpendicular lines
halves	1/2	quadrilateral	isosceles right triangle
quarters	1/4	triangle	octagon
eighths	1/8	length	width
sixteenths	1/16	parallel lines	line of symmetry

*Additional Activities:

1. **Calculate** the **area** and **volume** of the Math in Motion box. Measure in customary and metric units.

AREA

A. What is the area of the base of the box?
Measure the length and width. A = lw
Area is measured in square units.
1) Round your answer to the nearest 10th.
 A = 23.4 in.^{2} (5.5 x 4.25 = 23.375)
2) Round to the nearest whole number.
 A = 23 square inches

VOLUME

B. What is the volume of the box?
Measure the length, width and height. V = lwh
Volume is measured in cubic units.
1) Round your answer to the nearest 10th.
 V = 49.7 in.^{3} (5.5 x 4.25 x 2.125= 49.671)
2) Round to the nearest whole number.
 V = 50 cubic inches

*Challenge Questions: 1) Find the **surface area** of the box. **Surface Area** = 2lw + 2lh + 2wh or SA = 2(lw + hl + hw). Why do you adjust the formula for this box? Use: SA = lw + 2lh + 2wh

2. Make a basket. Fold a piece of paper lengthwise and staple a handle to the sides.

Box

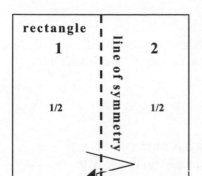

1 Start with a rectangle, white side up. Fold in half lengthwise (Book Fold). Unfold.

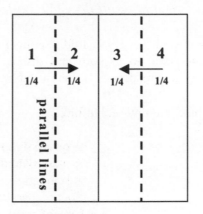

2 Bring longer edges to meet at the center crease (Cupboard Door Fold).

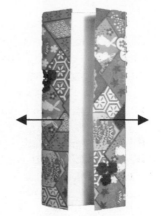

3 Unfold.

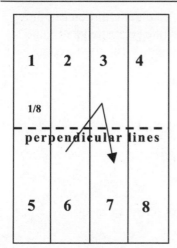

4 Fold in half widthwise (Book Fold). Unfold.

5 Bring shorter edges to meet at the center crease. This time leave the folds in.

isosceles triangle or 45° right triangle

6 At each corner, bring the folded edge to lie along the nearest crease to form a triangle. **Note:** Folded edges do NOT reach the centerline.

7 Fold the rectangular borders, one up and one down, as far as you can over the triangles to lock them down in place.

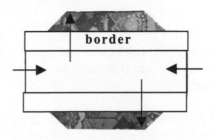

8 Place a thumb under each of the rectangular borders and pull them apart. The ends of the model will fold upward to form the sides of a box. Pinch the corners of the box to shape.

9 Voila! A finished box! Make another for a lid. Connect them together.

How to Fold a Box

I have all the right angles.

Explore the patterns on the paper each time you fold. Younger children can trace the place with their fingers or crayons. Give students time to explore and discover math concepts and vocabulary. The questions are in italics. Some suggested responses are on the right.

1. Fold the **whole** rectangle in half lengthwise. Unfold.

What is a rectangle?	A **quadrilateral** that has four right angles.
What is a quadrilateral?	A quadrilateral is a geometric figure with four sides.
What is a right angle?	A right angle measures 90°.
Name other quadrilaterals.	Square, parallelogram, rhombus, trapezoid.
What kind of line is it?	**Line of symmetry.**
What is a line of symmetry?	A line of folding so that the two parts of a figure match (congruent).
How many rectangles do you see all together?	Three.

Write the numbers 1 and 2 in each section of the paper model (see Step #1). Younger children can draw stars or apples to correspond with the numbers. Explore concepts like one-to-one correspondence and to distinguish between right and left. Older children can write fractions in each part. Write the fraction $\frac{1}{2}$.

Discuss parts of a fraction. In $\frac{1}{2}$, 1 is the numerator and 2 is the denominator.

2. Bring longer edges to meet at the center crease (Cupboard Door Fold). Unfold.

How many equal parts are there?	Four. Write in each part $\frac{1}{4}$.
What kind of line do you see?	Vertical lines.
What is another name for these lines?	Parallel lines.
What are parallel lines?	Lines that never intersect (cross or meet).

3. Fold in half widthwise. Unfold.

How many equal parts is the paper divided into?	Eight. Write in each part $\frac{1}{8}$.
What kind of lines do you see?	Perpendicular lines. Trace the lines.
What are perpendicular lines?	Lines that intersect and form right angles.

4. Bring shorter edges to meet at the center crease. Unfold. Discover a grid. The number grid offers many opportunities to explore and investigate number patterns and relationships: place value, counting, symbol recognition, comparing greater than and less, multiples of 2, 3, 4 and powers of 2, 4. Analyze the data and graph the results.

Unfold the paper. How many parts do you see?	Sixteen. Write in each part $\frac{1}{16}$.

5. Place the paper with the width at the top (*see diagram step #5*). Write the numbers 1-16 in each part. Younger children can practice counting backwards, forwards, skip counting by 2s and 4s. Practice adding or multiplying the rows and columns. Calculate mentally or with paper and pencil. Check your work with a calculator.

Put a square around the odd numbers. **☐1** **3, 5, 7, 9, 11, 13, 15.**

Circle the even numbers. **②** **4, 6, 8, 10, 12, 14, 16.**

Discover even + even numbers will always give an even number. **Example:** $2 + 4 = 6$.
Even + odd numbers will always give an odd number. **Example:** $2 + 3 = 5$.
Odd + odd numbers will always give an even number. **Example:** $3 + 5 = 8$.
Allow students to experiment, make predictions, test, justify and prove their work.
Ask students to draw or write about how they would explain their answers. Share observations.

Discuss prime and composite numbers.
What is a prime number?

A prime number is a whole number that is greater than 1 and has *exactly* two factors, 1 and itself. One is neither prime nor composite.

Place the letter "P" over all the prime numbers.
What is unique about the number 2?

2, 3, 5, 7, 11, 13.
It is the only even prime number.

What is a composite number?

A composite number is a whole number that is greater than 1 and has *more* than two factors.

Place the letter "C" over all the composite numbers. Extend to 100.

4, 6, 8, 9, 10, 12, 14, 15, 16.

Investigate number patterns. See *vertical* and *diagonal* number patterns.
What is the pattern for 1, 5, 9, 13?
Name or write the next 10 numbers in the series. Look for other patterns.

They all increase by the number 4.
17, 21, 25, 29, 33, 37, 41, 45, 49, and 53.

Compare numbers. Explore greater than and less than. Write 5 number sentences. Use the greater than > and less than < symbols. Example: Seven is less than nine. Write $7 < 9$.

6. Refold step #5. At each corner, bring the folded edge to lie along the nearest crease line.
    Note: The folded edges DO NOT reach the crosswise centerline.

What shape do you see? Triangle. Isosceles right triangle.
How many sides does the whole shape have? Eight.
What is the name of the shape? Octagon.
Is the octagon a regular or irregular shape? The octagon is irregular.
If all angles are equal and all sides are equal, then it is **regular**, otherwise it is **irregular.**

7. Fold the rectangular borders over the triangle. Repeat on the other side.

8. GENTLY open the sides to form a box. Pinch the corners to shape.

9. Voila! A finished box. Make another one the same size for a top and connect them together.

This model is suitable for all ages. The final assembly can be challenging, but with practice it will become easier to do.

Strand: Geometry ● Spatial Sense ● Language Arts

Materials: 8.5 x 11 inch rectangle (notebook or copy paper, recycle flyers)
Scissor ✂

Concepts and Vocabulary:

rectangle	**quadrilateral**	**line of symmetry**
vertical line	**length**	**width**
fractions	**whole**	**halves**
quarters	**eighths**	**perpendicular lines**
right angle	**midpoint**	**edge**

Additional Activities:

1. Make journal writing a part of your math class: write numerals, number facts, multiplication tables, formulas (see *Math Journals,* p. 89). Calculate all the possibilities: "Back to School Night" invitation, sketching, poetry, creative writing, spelling lists, and homework notebook.

2. For younger children, use the journal as an alphabet or picture word book. Students can draw or paste a picture above the new words. Make a list of the ways we use numbers and illustrate: age, weight, height, tell time, phone numbers, count change, measure items. See: www.literacycenter.net.

3. April is National Mathematics Education Month. Contact the National Council of Teachers of Mathematics (NCTM). Request a catalog and ask about FREE resources. Decorate your room with math posters and stickers. Display a Math in Motion exhibit in your classroom, school or local library. Ask your local newspapers/radio/TV to highlight this special event.

National Council of Teachers of Mathematics (NCTM)
1906 Association Drive
Reston, Virginia 22091
☎ 1-800-235-7566 ➤ www.nctm.org

Journal

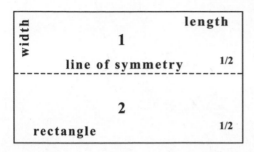

1 Start with a rectangle. Place the length (long edges) at the top and bottom. Fold in half lengthwise (Book Fold). Unfold.

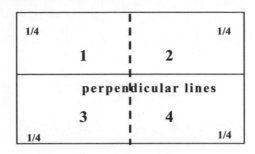

2 Fold in half widthwise (Book Fold). Do not unfold.

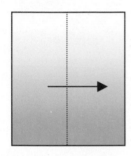

3 Fold the left side over to meet the right side (Book Fold). **Crease steps 3 and 4 sharply!**

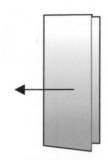

4 Unfold the last step. Repeat step 3 on the back. Unfold.

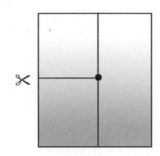

5 Cut along the centerline from the **folded** side to the midpoint.

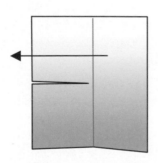

6 Unfold.

7 Fold the top edge down to the bottom again.

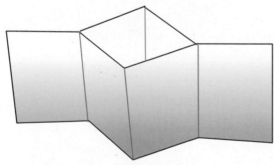

8 Push together to form a book, using the folds you have made. It creates a booklet with 8 pages.

51

9 Write your way into math! Mathematics + Writing = Success.

Jumping Frog

This popular action model will delight all ages. It requires a little more coordination. Can you make the frog jump into the box (see p. 47)?

Strand: Geometry • Measurement • Science • Language Arts

Materials: 3" x 5" green index card, card stock or a stiff rectangle

Alternative: Go Green. After students master the index card, challenge them to *recycle* smaller sizes like business cards or paint chips.

Concepts and Vocabulary:

plane	**rectangle**	**line segment**	**triangle**
perpendicular lines	**intersect**	**right angle**	**pentagon**

Additional Activities:

1. There are almost 4,000 different kinds of frogs and toads in the world. The Goliath is the world's largest frog with a body as big as a football. One of the smallest frogs found in the Cuban Rain Forest is no bigger than the eraser on your pencil! Study the life cycle of frogs. Find out more about these LEAPING amphibians at *All About Frogs:* www.allaboutfrogs.org.

2. Scientists from all over the world recently realized there are far fewer frogs than ever before. Frogs need puddles and ponds to hatch their eggs, but these places are often polluted. Start by making small changes in the classroom and at home. Join *Animal Crusaders* and protect the environment *(see Resources,* p. 116). Celebrate Earth Day, April 22 and make it a part of your life — every day. Find out what some classrooms and groups are working on to help our planet at *Teaching Green:* www.planetpals.com/thinkgreen.html.

3. Read *The Celebrated Jumping Frog of Calaveras County* by Mark Twain. The longest recorded jump of an *origami* frog is 5 ft. 10 in. (1.78 m). Experiment with different size paper frogs. What size frog jumps the farthest? Organize a Frog Jumping Olympics. Measure the length of your jumps and record the best distance out of two. Tabulate and graph the results. *What computation method should you use to answer the following questions?* **A)** Find the total distance Tamika's frog jumped. **B)** For Trial 1, how much farther did Jason's frog jump than Kenji's frog? **C)** Find the average lengths of the jumps in Trial 1. Results and answers appear in the data file tables below.

Frog-Jumping Contest

Student	Trial 1	Trial 2
Kenji	$3\frac{5}{8}$ in	5 in.
Tamika	$5\frac{7}{16}$ in.	$2\frac{1}{4}$ in.
Jason	$5\frac{3}{4}$ in.	$4\frac{1}{4}$ in.

Answers:
A) Tamika's frog jumped a total of $7\frac{11}{16}$ in.
B) Jason's frog jumped $2\frac{1}{8}$ inches farther than Kenji's frog.
C) The average length of the jumps in Trial 1 = $4\frac{15}{16}$ in.

Jumping Frog

1 **CREASE STEPS 1-3 SHARPLY!** Fold in half lengthwise. Unfold. Fold the top right corner over to the left edge (*AB*). Unfold.

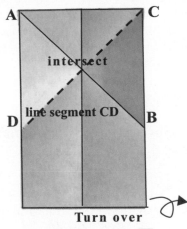

2 Repeat on the other side (*CD*). Unfold. Trace the letter 'X' with a pencil. Turn the card over.

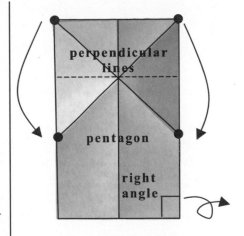

3 Fold the top of the 'X' down to the bottom of the 'X'. Unfold. Turn the card over.

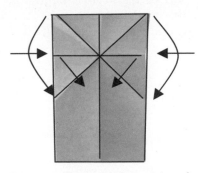

4 Put your finger in the center of the 'X' and the sides will pop up. The whole next move is done on creases made in steps 1-3. Push the sides toward the center (see the arrows) as the top collapses into a triangle.

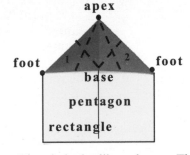

5 Now it looks like a house. The tip of the triangle will be the frog's nose (apex). The two side triangles will be the feet. Fold the side point (foot) of triangle #1 up to the top point (apex) of the triangle. Repeat on triangle #2 to form a square.

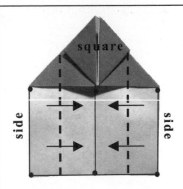

6 It looks like a house. Fold the sides of the house to the vertical line of symmetry (centerline).

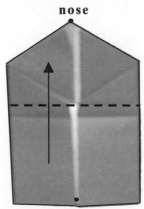

7 **CREASE SEPTS #7-8 LIGHTLY-** this is the spring action. GENTLY fold the bottom edge up to the nose.

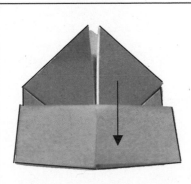

8 **CREASE LIGHTLY!** GENTLY fold back the top layer to match the folded edge at the bottom.

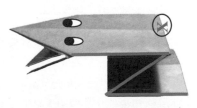

9 To make the frog jump, lightly press down on the frog's back, 'X' then let go. **Note:** The letter 'Z' formed by the side edge. This is the spring action that causes the frog to jump. Stretch it out and fold back lightly as needed to improve jump.

How to Fold a Jumping Frog

It's not easy being green. - Kermit the Frog

When green is all there is to be, it could make you wonder why,
but why wonder why? Wonder, I am green and it'll do fine, it's
beautiful! And I think it's what I want to be.

--The Sesame Street Book and Record,
'Green' ©1970 Jonico Music, Inc.

Suggestion: Discuss the characteristics of a **rectangle** and **plane** figure. A plane is a flat surface that continues infinitely in all directions. See *How to Fold the Box* to extend the lesson on rectangles, (p. 48).

1. Place the rectangle on the table **vertically**. Fold in half lengthwise. Unfold. Fold the right top edge over to the left edge. Unfold.

   What kind of line does this fold create?   **Line segment**.

   What is a line segment?   A line segment is part of a line that begins at one **point** and ends at another point. It is named by its two endpoints. Label it line segment AB or $\overline{AB}$.

2. Repeat on the other side. Unfold. Label it line segment *CD*. Trace the letter "X" on the card with a pencil to distinguish between the front and back.

   What kind of lines do $\overline{AB}$ and $\overline{CD}$ form?   They form **perpendicular lines**.

   What are perpendicular lines?   These are lines that **intersect** (cross) and form **right angles.**

   What is a right angle?   A right angle measures 90^0.
   How many right angles do the perpendicular   Four.
   lines form? What is the sum of all the angles? 360^0.

3. Turn the card over. Point to the top of the "X." Point to the bottom of the "X." Take the top of the "X" and fold it down to the bottom of the "X" (CREASE SHARPLY, 3-4x). Unfold. The crease will **bisect** line segments AB and CD or the "X." Turn the card over.

   Unfold all the steps and study the patterns.
   *How many **triangles** are there?*   Can you find all 16 triangles?

4. Poke your finger in the center of the "X" and the sides will pop-up. The whole next move is done on pre-existing creases from steps 1-3. Place the index of your fingertips on the sides of the bisecting horizontal line where the arrows are pointing. Push the sides toward the center as the top collapses into a triangle. It looks like a house (See step #5).

How many sides does this polygon have?   Five.

What is a five sided figure called?   **Pentagon**.

Trace the pentagon with your finger and label the sides.

5. Fold the right side point (foot) of the triangle up to the top point or apex of the triangle. Repeat on the left side. The **apex** the triangle (top point) will be the frog's nose. The two triangles on the sides will be its feet.

   What shape do these triangles create?   **Square**.

6. Fold the sides of the house to the **vertical line of symmetry** (centerline) to narrow the card.

7. **WARNING:** DO NOT CREASE STEPS #7 and #8 SHARPLY. This is the spring action that makes the frog jump. GENTLY fold the bottom straight edge of the card up to the apex.

8. GENTLY fold the top edge down in half towards you (creates a pleat) to match the folded edge at the bottom.

9. To make the frog jump, *lightly* press down on the frog's back and let go.
   A) Make two and play leapfrog. **B)** Create an obstacle course—over mountains of books, pencils, erasers and miniature ponds created from foil paper. Use masking tape to set up a starting point and finishing line.

Is your school and home a "**green**" and healthy place to work and live? Find out more about "green" programs. Visit these eco-friendly websites: earthday.wilderness.org/, www.earth911.org, www.greenteacher.com, www.recycling-revolution.com/, www.kidsplanet.org, www.planetpals.org. Email us your "green" ideas and projects and we will post it to our website to share with others. ✉ Email: info@mathinmotion.com

55

How to Make
a Square from a Rectangle

Method #1

Fold the left bottom corner to the opposite side to form a triangle.

Cut along the vertical line of the rectangle. Unfold. The paper is now a square.
Alternative: *Without a scissor*, fold the rectangular portion back and forth several times. Place one hand against the triangle. Carefully separate the rectangular portion with your other hand.

The rectangular strip left over can be used for making smaller squares or other models: Make a 1) heart 🖤 (p. 43) or 2) a handle for a basket. To shape a handle: Fold in half lengthwise (Book Fold). Unfold. Fold the sides to the center (Cupboard Door Fold). Staple it to the sides of the box (p. 46).

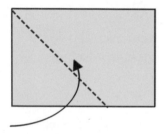

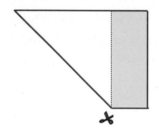

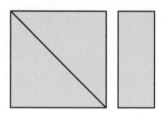

Method #2

For a square without a diagonal crease, place two identical sheets of rectangular paper as shown. Cut the bottom sheet along the raw edge of the top sheet.

The sheet underneath is now square. For a second square, turn both layers over and cut the larger sheet using the raw edge of the square as a guide.

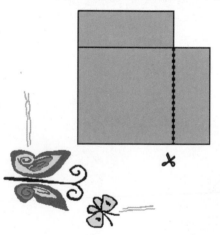

This fishy model is easy and good for beginners. Have a whale of a time!

FUN FACTS: The whistle of the blue whale is the loudest sound produced by any animal at 188 decibels.

Strand: Geometry ● Spatial Sense ● Patterns ● Connections ● Science

Materials: A 6-inch or larger square (15 cm), start white side up

Concepts & Vocabulary:

square	quadrilateral	triangle	scalene triangle
congruent	vertical	center	isosceles right triangle
right	left	point	line of symmetry

Additional Activities:

1. How many ways can a square be divided into 4 equal parts?

2. Make a whale as a Father's Day card for a "Whale of a Dad." Use as name tags for the first day of school "a school of fish" or "Back to School" Night.

3. Did you know whales sing? Nobody knows for sure, but perhaps they are singing the blues. Listen to Paul Winter's, "Lullaby from the Great Mother Whale for the Baby Seal Pups," *Concert for the Earth, Live at the United Nations.* Younger children will enjoy singing "Baby Beluga" with *Raffi in Concert.*

4. Read *A Thousand Pails of Water* by R. Roy (K-2), *Whale of a Tale* by Barbara Pearl (PreK-2) includes a study guide available at: www.mathinmotion.com/studyguides, *Humphrey, The Wayward Whale* by E. Callenbach (K-6) and other stories about fish-like mammals (dolphins, manatees, porpoises, seals, and walruses). The *Whale's Stomach* lesson plan (Grades 4+) by the Institute for Humane Education raises awareness about ocean pollution and its effect on sea animals. See lesson plan at: www.info@mathinmotion.com/whalesstomach. To adopt a whale, contact:

Greenpeace
1436 U Street, N.W.
Washington, D.C. 20009
1-800-456-4029
www.greenpeace.org

Save the Whales
1192 Waring Street
Seaside, CA 93955
1-800-942-5365
www.savethewhales.org

Whale

square

quadrilateral

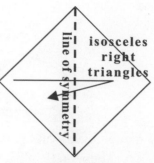

isosceles right triangles

line of symmetry

1. Place a 6-inch square sheet of paper on the table so it looks like a diamond.

2. Fold the left point over to meet the right point (fold in half). Unfold.

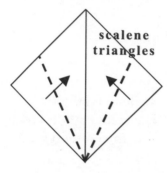

scalene triangles

apex

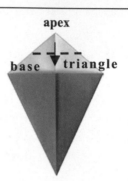

base triangle

3. Fold the lower left and right sides to meet at the vertical line of symmetry.

4. It looks like a kite. Now fold the apex (top point) down to the base line to form a small triangle.

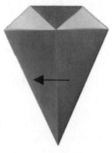

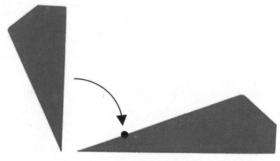

5. Fold the right side over to meet the left side (fold in half).

6. Put your finger on the bottom point as you turn the whale sideways.

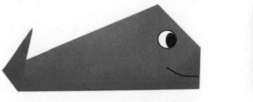

7. Fold the end point up to make a tail.

8. Draw a happy face. Have a whale of a day! For a surprise, rotate the whale—open to stand and create a penguin instead.

For an animated version of the *Whale,* see:
www.mathinmotion.com

How to Fold a Whale

1. Place a square sheet of paper on the table so it looks like a diamond shape.

   What shape is the paper? **Square.**

   How many sides does a square have? **4 sides.**

   What else can you say about the sides? The sides are the same or **congruent.**

   Another name for a four sided figure is **quadrilateral** (see *Quadrilaterals*, p. 60).

   Can you think of other quadrilaterals? Rectangle, parallelogram, rhombus, trapezoid.

   Name other quadrilaterals in the room. Book, chalkboard, desk, table, window.

2. Fold the right point over to the left point. Unfold.

   *What is the **vertical** line?* **Line of Symmetry.**

   What is a line of symmetry? A line of folding so that the two halves of a figure match.

   What shape did it create? **Triangles.**

   What kind of triangles? **Isosceles right triangles.**

   What is an isosceles right triangle? It has two sides that are congruent and a square corner.

3. Fold the lower left and right sides to meet the center crease. Unfold the paper and discover more triangles.

   What kind of triangles? **Scalene** triangles.

   What are scalene triangles? They have no congruent sides.

   How many triangles are there? Six. Refold the model.

   What does it look like? It looks like a kite or an ice cream cone.

4. Fold the apex (top point) down to the base (widest part of the kite) to form a small triangle▲. Unfold.

   How many triangles are there? 11. See triangles ABD, ABC, ADC, AEG, AEF, AGF, AEH, AGH, EFH, GFH, EHG.

   What other shapes do you see on the kite? Trapezoid. Quadrilateral.

5. Refold the model. Fold the **right** side over to meet the **left** side.

6. Put your finger on the bottom point as you turn the whale sideways.

7. Fold the **point** up to make a tail. Draw a happy face. Have a whale of a day! ☺

Quadrilateral

Quad-ri-lat-er-al is Latin for a figure that has four sides. "Quad," means four and "lateral," means side. Find other quadrilaterals.

1) Look for objects in the room that are similar in shape.
2) Trace the geometric shapes below and draw another one.
3) See *Tangram Puzzles*, p. 98 and make a quadrilateral.

1. **Square** - a figure that has four right angles and four sides of equal length. Every square is a rectangle.

2. **Rectangle** - a quadrilateral that has four right angles. Every rectangle is a parallelogram.

3. **Parallelogram** - a quadrilateral that has two pairs of parallel sides and two pairs of congruent sides.

4. **Rhombus** - a parallelogram that has four congruent sides. Every rhombus is a parallelogram.

5. **Trapezoid** - a quadrilateral that has exactly one pair of parallel sides.

Square Motion

There are many ways to fold a square into four equal parts.

Explore some of the possibilities with the squares below.

Materials: paper / pencil/ ruler/ three squares

✎**Note to Teacher:** See *Enter the Fold*, p. 23

1. **How can a square be divided into four equal parts?**
2. **Describe the folds and list your observations.**
3. **Fold the square patterns.**
4. **Create your own geometric designs.**
5. **Color the square patterns.**

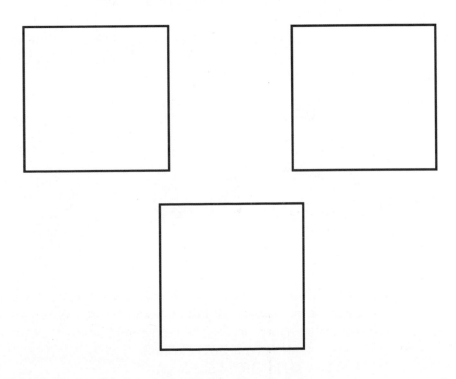

Wolf or Fox

The wolf's ears are challenging. Work in small groups or demonstrate to several students. Then ask them to assist other children in the room.

Strand: Geometry ● Spatial Sense ● Language Arts ● Science

Materials: A 6-inch or larger square (15 cm) ● Crayons or markers

Concepts and Vocabulary:

square	**line of symmetry**	**triangle**	**right angle**
point	**isosceles right triangle**	**edge**	**side**

Additional Activities:

1. Make a wolf mask using a 12-inch square. Cut out holes for the 👁👁 eyes. Staple an elastic band to hold the mask in place on the child's face.

2. Idioms: This activity develops comprehension of language arts skills. Invite students to illustrate the literal and figurative meanings of the following idioms. Make up your own idioms. Display on a bulletin board.

   1. sly as a fox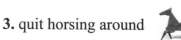

   2. let the cat out of the bag

   3. quit horsing around

   4. it's raining cats and dogs

   5. a frog in my throat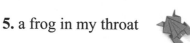

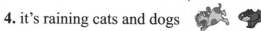

3. Sponsor a canis lupus pambasileuses (wolves)! Learn more about what you can do to conserve and protect wildlife. Join Wolf Haven International and receive a certificate. Membership includes your wolf's name, photo, biography and bookmark. Contact:

Wolf Haven International
3111 Offut Lake Road
Tenino, Washington 98589
www.wolfhaven.org
☎ 1-800-448-9653

Wolf

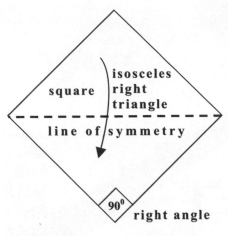

1 Start with a square, white side up so it looks like a diamond. Fold the top point down to meet the bottom point (forms a triangle).

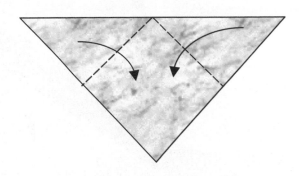

2 Fold the left and right points down to meet the bottom point (forms a square).

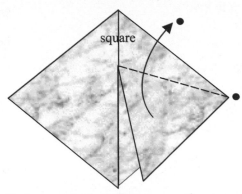

3 Put your index finger on the top point. Fold the lower right point of the triangle up to the dot to make the ears.

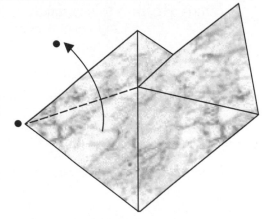

4 Repeat with the lower left point.

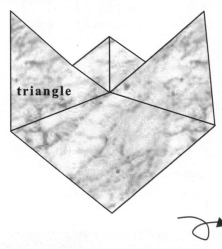

5 Turn over.

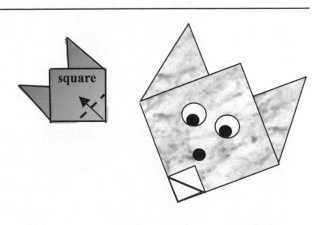

6 Look at the lower point. There are two layers. Fold only the top layer up along the dotted line to make the mouth. Draw eyes and nose.

Pig

To open and close the pig's mouth, place your thumbs on its ears and your fingers on the back of its head. Move your hands together and apart.

Strand: Geometry ● Spatial Sense ● Language Arts

Materials: A 6-inch square, (15 cm) white side up
Crayons or markers

Concepts and Vocabulary:

square	**line of symmetry**	**triangle**
point	**isosceles right triangle**	**edge**

Additional Activities:

1. Make the cat, dog and other *Math in Motion* animals. Discuss animal sounds.

2. Prepare a diorama showing animals in their natural environment. Read or watch *Charlotte's Web* by E. B. White. Fold animals to dramatize the story.

3. Make three pig puppets and a wolf to illustrate *The Three Little Pigs* (Brothers Grimm). Glue the back of the paper puppets to popsicle sticks. Many children's fables and stories give the wolf a bad name. Describe what is wrong with the way the wolf is portrayed in the story. Retell it. Give the wolf a new personality and the story a new twist. Explain that *The Three Little Pigs* has many different versions and each story is written a little differently. Engage students in a discussion to compare and contrast the stories. Be kind to all creatures.

4. Use analogies to develop auditory associations and vocabulary. Read the analogies aloud. Emphasize the key words. Make up other animal analogies.

Mothers and their Babies

Dog is to **puppy** as cat is to **(kitten).**   Bear is to **cub** as deer is to **(fawn).**

Pig is to **piglet** as frog is to **(tadpole).**   Wolf is to **pup** as whale is to **(calf).**

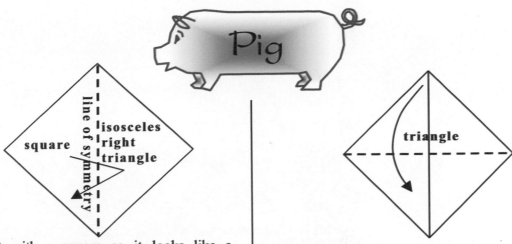

Pig

1 Start with a square so it looks like a diamond. Fold in half so that the left point meets the right point (triangle). Unfold.

2 Fold the top point down to meet the bottom point.

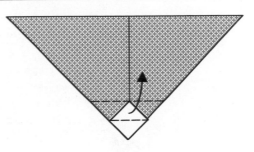

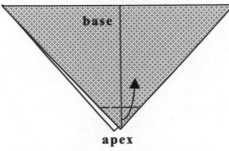

3 Now there are two layers. Fold the top layer up to make a small triangle.

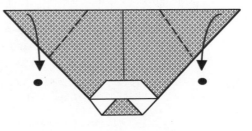

4 Fold the small triangle up again to form the snout.

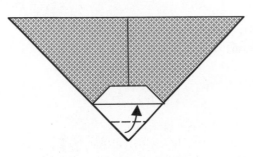

5 Fold the bottom point up and tuck it inside.

6 Fold the right and left points down to the dots to form the ears. These ears will cover part of the pig's face.

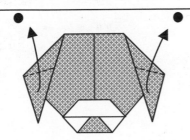

7 Fold the points of the ears up to the dots.

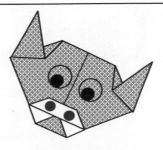

8 Draw eyes and nostrils. Oink! Oink!

Candy Cane

This is a fun holiday model. To shape the candy cane, roll the paper tightly around a pencil. Then slip the pencil out to shape.

Strand: **Geometry** • **Spatial Sense**
Language Arts • **Social Studies**

Materials: **A 6-8-inch square, white side up or precut squares from holiday gift wrap. Color or draw a pattern on one side of the paper. Tape or glue (optional).**

Concepts and Vocabulary:

square   equal   quadrilateral   "L"   vertical
opposite   side   horizontal   corner

Additional Activities:

1. Wrapped in Wishes: 1) Write a wish for someone special on the white side of the paper, (see step #3) or 2) Make a list of all the words that start with the letter "L": love, life, like, learn. The words will appear on the outside when you roll it up.

2. Discuss how other cultures celebrate holidays or festivals: Mexican-piñata, Chinese-New Year dragon, Jewish-dreidles, Japanese-tea ceremony, Irish-shamrock, African-Kwanza.

3. Discuss the multiple meanings of the word cane: sugar, candy, walking aid for injured, handicapped or elderly people.

PEACE ON EARTH

Candy Cane

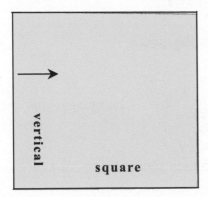

1 Start with a square, white side up. Fold the left vertical side over about ½ inch.

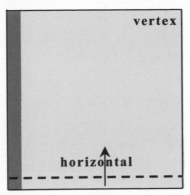

2 Fold the bottom horizontal edge up about ½ inch to form the letter "L".

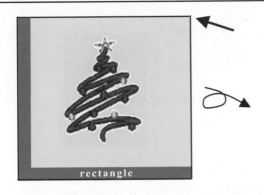

3 Hold the top right corner on the white side and turn the paper over. **DON'T LET GO!**

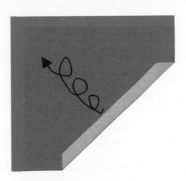

4 Roll the corner you are holding to the opposite corner. **Optional:** Use a pencil to roll it around the paper and slip it out to shape.

5 Pinch the center point closed. Use glue or tape as needed to hold the paper in place. Press the top half flat. Curl it around your finger to form a hook.

6 *Happy Holidays!*

This practical model is FUNctional.

Strand: Geometry • Spatial Sense • Science • Cup Language Arts

Material: paper square, 6 inch or larger, white side up
Alternative: Recycle 8.5 x 11 inch paper to make an 8.5 x 8.5 inch square (see p. 56).

Concepts and Vocabulary:

square	**quadrilateral**	**triangle**	**side**
scalene	**horizontal**	**diagonal**	**edge**
opposite	**symmetry**	**isosceles**	**bottom**
layer	**trapezoid**	**pocket (opening)**	

Additional Activities:

1. Discuss what you could put inside your cup: healthy snacks, fruit,  popcorn, peanuts, raisins. Nutrition is essential to health. According to the National Science Education Standards, students should understand how the body uses food and how various foods contribute to health and growth (see, www.nsta.org).

2. Will the cup hold liquid? Test over a sink or plastic container. Promote scientific inquiry. Communicate investigations and explanations. **A)** Experiment with making the cup out of different paper materials: wax or freezer paper, lunch bags, brown paper bags, typing, construction, computer, or notebook paper. **B)** Create a table for the data. **C)** Compare your results. **D)** Name other items that hold liquid: glass, bowl, bucket, bottle, pot, jar.

3. Save a bug  in your cup and set it free. Read the delightful children's story, *I Was Walking Down the Road* by Sarah E. Barchas (K-2).

4. Make a life-size model hat out of newspaper approximately 20-inch square (adjust the dimensions as needed) to fit a child's head. Be creative. Decorate with paper scraps, felt, tissue, crepe paper, pastas, noodles. Color or paint your hat the school colors.

Cup

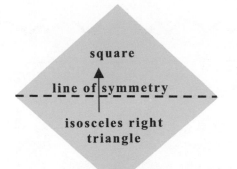

1 Start with a square, white side up. Fold in half along the dotted line.

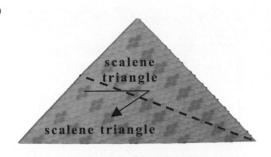

2 Fold the right edge of the top layer to the bottom edge. Unfold.

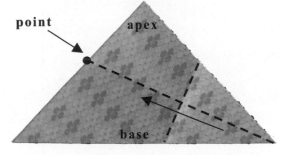

3 Fold the bottom right corner along the dotted line to the point on the opposite side. Crease sharply.

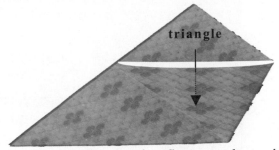

4 See the pocket in the flap you have just made? Fold the top (front) triangle above the pocket downward and slide the triangle into the pocket of the cup as far as it will go.

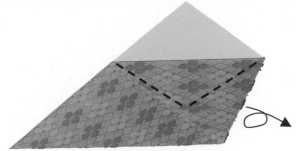

5 Flap is now locked into place. Turn over.

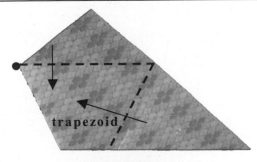

6 Repeat step #3 and #4.

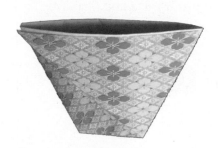

7 Finished cup!

8 Made of newspaper about 23 inches square, the cup becomes a hat.

Picture Frame

This model makes a great gift! It requires accuracy in folding.

FUN FACTS: How many times can you fold a piece of paper in half? In January 2002, when Britney Gallivan was a junior in high school, she set a new world record of folding a piece of paper in half from eight times to twelve times! See: www.sciencenewsforkids.org.

Strand: Geometry ● Spatial Sense ● Patterns ● Language Arts

Materials: A 6-inch or larger square, colored on one side.

> **Hint:** A 6-inch square fits a 3-inch picture. Experiment with rectangular shapes and frame your favorite photos.

Concepts and Vocabulary:

square	**quadrilateral**	**equal**
side	**halves**	**quarters**
triangle	**right triangle**	

Additional Activities:

1. Unfold the picture frame and explore paper patterns. Discover smaller squares within larger squares. Find triangles within triangles.  Trace the outline of the shapes with your pencil or markers. How many squares can you find? How many triangles? Number each one. Color squares blue. Color triangles red. Create color patterns.

2. Draw a picture inside the frame as a gift for mother or father's day, birthdays,  celebrations or special occasions.

3. Insert students' baby photos  in origami picture frames and display in class. Have fun guessing who's who. Number the frames. Write the student's name and number on a separate sheet. Compare your answers.

4. Discuss different kinds of frames like picture, door and window.

Picture Frame

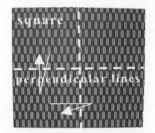

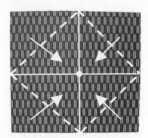

1 Start with a square, colored side up. Next, fold the paper in half. Then, fold the paper in half again widthwise. Unfold.

2 Fold each corner to the midpoint.

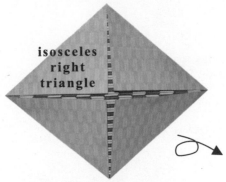

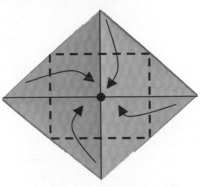

3 It looks like this. Turn over.

4 Fold each corner to the midpoint again

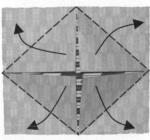

5 Now it looks like this. Turn it over again.

6 Starting at the midpoint, fold each inside corner of each square to the outside corner forming small triangles.

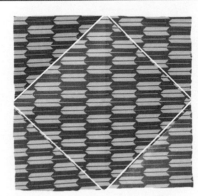

7 Turn the picture frame over.

8 Unfold opposite triangular flaps (see arrows) so that they are perpendicular to the side edges of the frame. It will lean slightly backward as the frame rests on the slanted edges of the flaps.

How to Make an Isosceles Right Triangle from a Square

Isosceles triangles have two sides the same length.

A right triangle has one square corner.

An isosceles right triangle has both.

Follow steps #1-3 to make an isosceles right triangle.

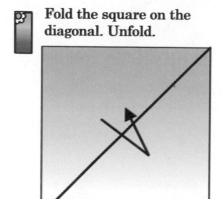 **1** Fold the square on the diagonal. Unfold.

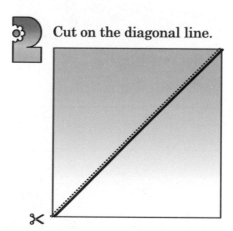 **2** Cut on the diagonal line.

 **3** Two isosceles right triangles.

This model is ideal for younger children. It only has a few steps and is easy to teach.

Strand: Geometry ● Spatial Sense ● Language Arts

Materials: Triangle. Cut a square on the diagonal to form 2 triangles.
Instruct students to "pair share," a term used when students work cooperatively toward a common goal. Allow time to explore. 1) Ask students to find a square shape by matching their triangle with another student. Discover that 2 isosceles right triangles = 1 square. (Fig. 1) 2) Make a larger triangle. (Fig. 2) 3) Place one triangle on top of another triangle to form a six-pointed star (Star of David, Fig. 3) 4) What other shapes can you make: parallelogram, butterfly, bowtie, sailboat, hour glass, pine tree?

Concepts and Vocabulary:

triangle	**isosceles right triangle**	**right**
apex (top)	**right angle**	**left**
base (bottom)	**side**	**up**
congruent	**edge**	**down**

Additional Activities:

1) Decorate the classroom by hanging up origami dogs on a clothesline. Write a poem on the back of the dog model or attach it to a short story.

2) Celebrate National Pet Week the first week of May. Be kind to *all* animals everyday. Glue popsicle sticks on the back of the origami dog and have a puppet show. Make up a play or read Steven Kellogg's series on *Pinkerton* (K-3).

3) Discuss different breeds of dogs like collie, dalmatian and greyhound. Write a report about your favorite kind of dog. Display on the bulletin board.

www.animalsvoice.com

Dog

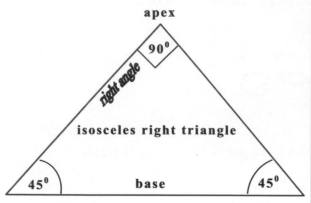

apex

90°

right angle

isosceles right triangle

45°   base   45°

1 Start with a triangle, white side up.

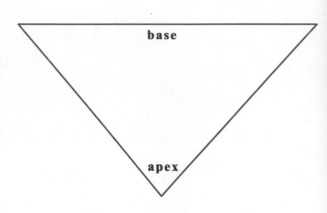

base

apex

2 Put the triangle on the table so the apex is pointing down.

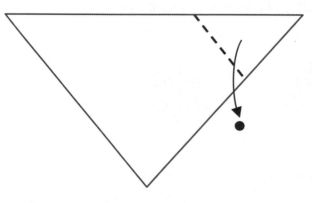

3 Fold one side down to make an ear.

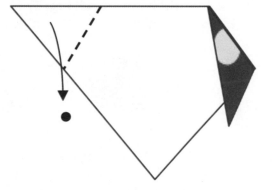

4 Repeat on the other side.

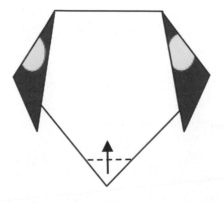

5 Fold the bottom point up to make a small triangle to form the mouth.

6 Bow-wow! Draw the dog's face. You have made a dog with floppy ears!

How to Fold a Dog

1. Start with a triangle shape. Discuss the characteristics of a triangle. Have students write the names of the terms on the paper triangle.

What is the top part of a triangle?	**Apex.**
What is the bottom part of a triangle?	**Base.**
How many sides does a triangle have?	Three.
Points? Angles? Vertices?	Three. Three. Three.
Are the sides of the triangle the same length?	Yes, two **sides** are exactly the same length (**congruent**).

Estimate the length of each side of the triangle. Then measure the sides of the triangle with both the standard and metric side of your ruler. How close did you get to your estimate?

What kind of triangle is it?	**Isosceles right triangle** (IRT).
What is an isosceles right triangle?	A triangle that has two **congruent** sides and one **right angle**.
What is a right angle?	**An angle that forms a square corner and measures 90^0.**
What do the other angles measure?	The other angles each measures **45^0**.
What is the sum of all the angles?	The sum of all the angles of a triangle is **180^0**.

Draw an isosceles right triangle. Measure the angles with a protractor and label them.
See the *Dog* diagram, step #1.

Make a trapezoid with three isosceles right triangles (IRT).

What shape can you make with six IRT?   Hexagon.

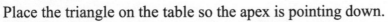

2. Place the triangle on the table so the apex is pointing down.

3. Fold the **right** side **down** to form an ear, as shown.

4. Repeat on the **left** side.

5. Fold the bottom point up into the shape of a small triangle to form a mouth.

6. Draw the dog's face. 1, 2, 3 (ichi, ni, san). Look how much fun math can be!!!

Math Word Search

Directions: Find the following math words.
Look vertical (up and down) and horizontal (across).

ANGLE   PERPENDICULAR
GEOMETRY   RECTANGLE
MATH   SQUARE
ORIGAMI   SYMMETRY
PARALLEL   TRIANGLE

Bonus Word: Can you find the word FUN?

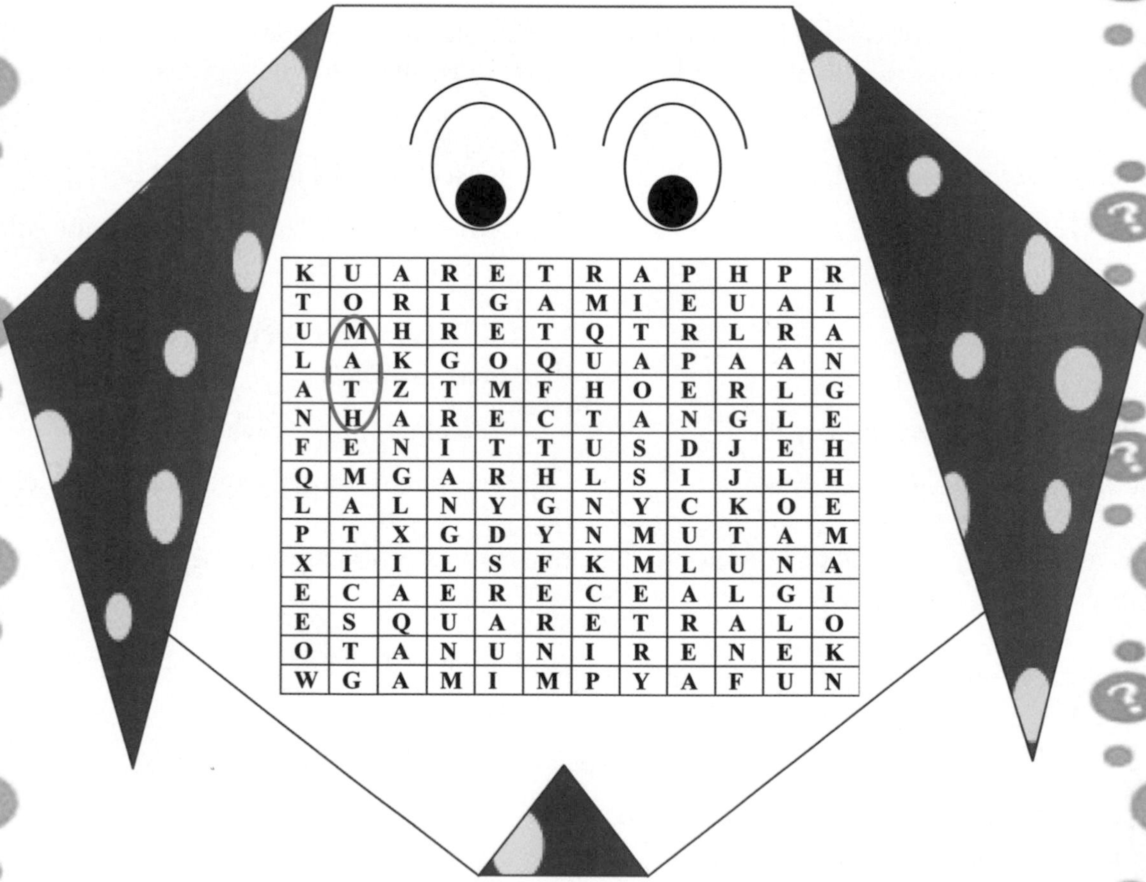

K	U	A	R	E	T	R	A	P	H	P	R
T	O	R	I	G	A	M	I	E	U	A	I
U	M	H	R	E	T	Q	T	R	L	R	A
L	A	K	G	O	Q	U	A	P	A	A	N
A	T	Z	T	M	F	H	O	E	R	L	G
N	H	A	R	E	C	T	A	N	G	L	E
F	E	N	I	T	T	U	S	D	J	E	H
Q	M	G	A	R	H	L	S	I	J	L	H
L	A	L	N	Y	G	N	Y	C	K	O	E
P	T	X	G	D	Y	N	M	U	T	A	M
X	I	I	L	S	F	K	M	L	U	N	A
E	C	A	E	R	E	C	E	A	L	G	I
E	S	Q	U	A	R	E	T	R	A	L	O
O	T	A	N	U	N	I	R	E	N	E	K
W	G	A	M	I	M	P	Y	A	F	U	N

76

Try-Angles

The right angle to solve a problem is the try-angle.

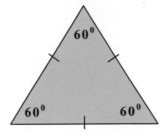

Explore different kinds of triangles. Triangles can be classified by the lengths of their sides. Draw a similar triangle next to it. Similar figures have the same shape and may or may not have the same size. Space is provided to the right.

☑ **Challenge Activity:** Use a protractor to measure and draw the angles. The sum of the angles in any triangle is 180°·

1. **Equilateral triangle** – All sides are equal.
   The triangles below are similar. See *How to Make an Equilateral Triangle from a Rectangle*, p. 79.

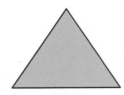

2. **Isosceles triangle** –At least two sides are equal. See *How to Make an Isosceles Right Triangle from a Square*, p.72. See *Dog, Cat, Sailboat*, pp. 73-84.

3. **Scalene triangle** – No sides are equal. See *Whale*, p. 58, step #3 for examples of scalene triangles.

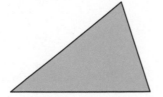

Triangle Tower

Circle the name of the triangle.

scalene   isosceles   **equilateral**

How many triangles can you find?

Color the triangles.

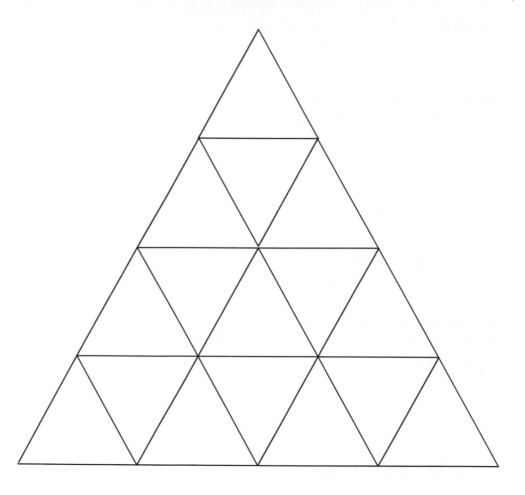

Answer: triangles

Write your answer inside the triangle.

How to Make an Equilateral Triangle from a Rectangle

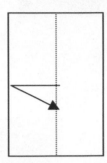

1. Start with an 8.5" x 11" rectangle. Fold in half lengthwise. Unfold.

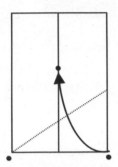

2. Fold from the bottom right corner up to the center line. Make sure the line also intersects (crosses) the bottom left corner.

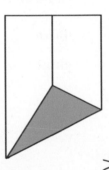

3. Turn over.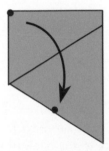

4. Fold the top edge to lie flush with the folded edge.

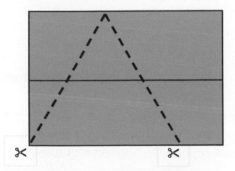

5. Unfold. Cut diagonal lines.

6. Wow! Color the equilateral triangle. Can you invent an origami model?

This model has very few steps and is easy for younger children.

Strand: Geometry ● Spatial Sense ● Language Arts ● Science

Materials: Triangle

> **Hint:** Cut a square on the diagonal to form two triangles.
> "Pair Share." See Material guidelines for *Dog*, p. 73.

Concepts and Vocabulary:

triangle	**isosceles right triangle**	**pentagon**
apex (top)	**base (bottom)**	**congruent (same)**
side	**up**	**down**
right	**left**	**point**

Additional Activities:

1. Read and dramatize *The Three Little Kittens* or Dr. Seuss, *Cat in the Hat* books. Glue popsicle sticks to the back of the model to make puppets.

2. Make other *Math in Motion* animals and discuss their differences. Compare and Contrast: 1) size 2) what they eat 3) where they live and 4) what sounds they make.

3. Make an animal mobile. See *How to Make an Origami Mobile,* p. 101.

4. Celebrate Halloween: Decorate the classroom with cat posters, place mats and centerpieces.

5. Volunteer at an animal shelter for a community service project. Adopt or provide a foster home for a pet. Discuss different breeds of cats like Burmese, Persian, Siamese. Write a report about your favorite kind of cat. Attach the origami cat to your report. Display on a clothesline in the classroom or bulletin board.

Cat

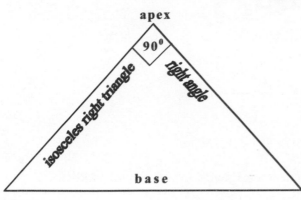

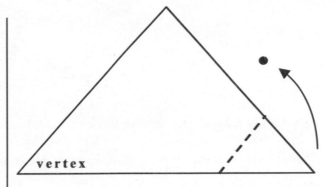

1 Begin with a triangle, white side up.

2 Fold one point up to the dot to make an ear.

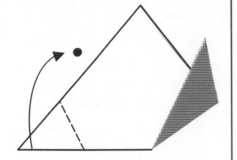

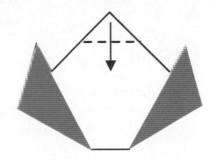

3 Repeat with the other point.

4 Now it looks like a tulip.

5 Fold the top point down to make another triangle.

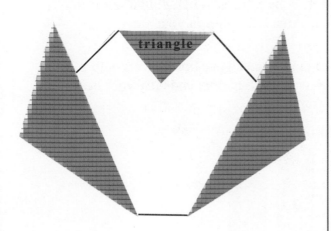

6 It looks like this.

7 Turn over. Meow! Draw a face and whiskers. Turn it over to find a dog (p. 74).

Sailboat

Ship ahoy mates! This action model is suitable for kids of all ages.

Strand: Geometry • Spatial Sense • Measurement • Language Arts • Social Studies

Materials: Begin with a triangle, white side up.

Hint: Cut a square on the diagonal to form 2 triangles.

Concepts and Vocabulary:

triangle	**side**	**base**	**apex**
point	**right triangle**	**halfway**	**angle**

Additional Activities:

1. Sail ahead with *Math in* Motion. Write your name on the sail. Use as name cards or as a prompt for a story. Decorate a bulletin board (seasonal). Glue the sailboat onto a greeting card and send to a friend or grandparent.

2. Columbus Day: Make three boats representing the Niña, Pinta and Santa María.

3. Thanksgiving: Discuss how the Pilgrims traveled to the New World. Examine the Thanksgiving story from both perspectives of the Pilgrim and Native American. Read *The Thanksgiving 1621: A New Look at Thanksgiving* by C. O'Neill Grace (ages 8-12) and *Giving Thanks: The 1621 Harvest Feast* by K. Waters (ages 7-12). Fold a sailboat to represent the Mayflower. Write a story about it. Attach the ship to your story.

4. Gently blow the sailboat across a table. Measure the distance your boat travels before it capsizes. Compare your results with a partner. Record the outcome and tally your best score out of three. Graph the results with a bar graph.

Sailboat Results
1) 2 inches
2) 5 inches
3) 3.5 inches

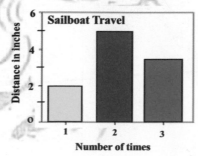

Sailboat

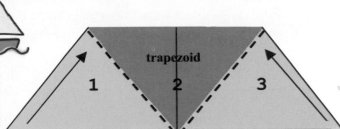

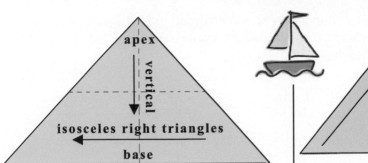

1 Begin with a triangle, white side up. Put the triangle on the table with the longest side toward you (base). Fold the triangle in half along the vertical dotted line. Unfold. Fold the top point (apex) down to the bottom edge (base) of the triangle (see step #2).

2 What shape do you see? Trapezoid. Now, fold Triangle 1 up along the dotted line. It covers part of the center of triangle 2. Repeat with triangle 3.

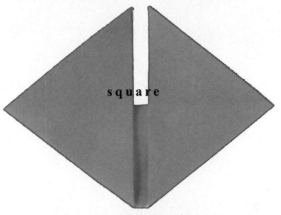

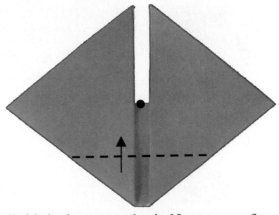

3 Now the two side triangles cover most of the center triangle (forms a square).

4 Fold the bottom point halfway up to form a small triangle (see black dot).

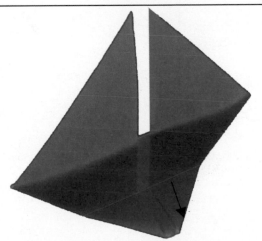

5 Pull the small triangle back halfway (toward you) to make a stand.

6 Turn it around to discover a sailboat. Sail ahead with *Math in Motion*.

Sailboat ▲ Tulip ▲ Dog

These diagrams illustrate how some shapes can be transformed into different models. Fold the sailboat base into a tulip and a dog. Challenge students to study the patterns in other diagrams and have fun creating original models.

Sailboat	Tulip	Dog
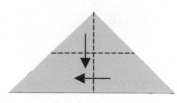 **1** Fold along the vertical dotted line. Unfold. Fold in half along the horizontal dotted line.	 **1** Unfold the sailboat. Study the patterns on the paper. Fold each bottom corner up along the dotted line.	 **1** Turn the tulip upside down. Fold the bottom point up along the dotted line.
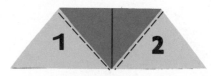 **2** Fold triangle 1 up along the diagonal dotted line. Repeat with triangle 2 to form a square.	 **2** Now you have a tulip. Draw a stem, decorate a card, personalize your stationery or create an Asian scroll.	 **2** Now you have a dog! Draw the dog's face. Turn it over to find a cat (p. 81).
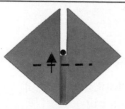 **3** Fold up along the dotted line to make a stand for the sailboat.		
 **4** Pull the small triangle halfway back (toward you) to make a stand.	Roll chopsticks at the top and bottom of the scroll and glue them around it.	Glue popsicle sticks to the back and make puppets.
 **5** Turn over to see your finished sailboat!		

Part VI

Cultural

&

Educational

Enrichment

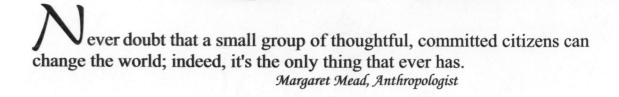

Never doubt that a small group of thoughtful, committed citizens can change the world; indeed, it's the only thing that ever has.

Margaret Mead, Anthropologist

Math in Motion

Color the crane for a world of peace.

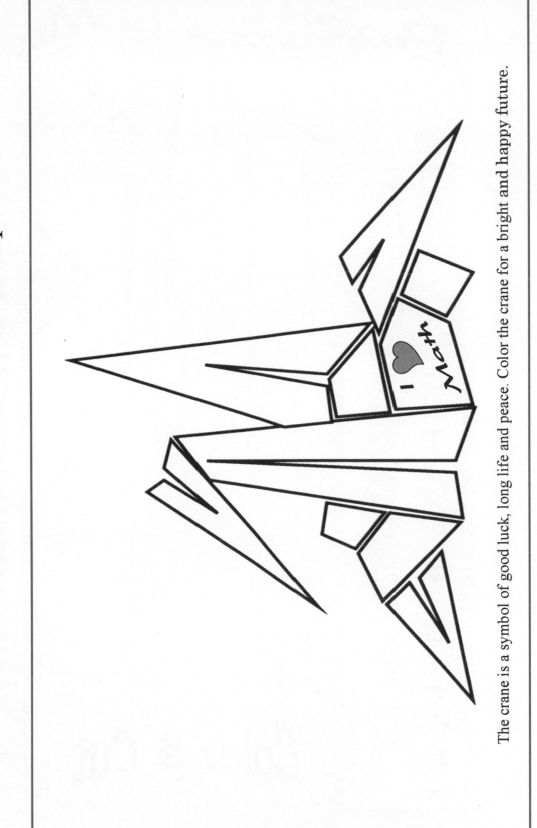

The crane is a symbol of good luck, long life and peace. Color the crane for a bright and happy future.

87

Book Marks

I ♥ Math in Motion

I ♥ Math

A lonely magician gains friends through the paper crane he brings to life. Read *Perfect Crane* by Anne Laurin.

I ♥ Math in Motion

The crane is an international symbol of peace and good-luck. Read *Sadako and the Thousand Paper Cranes* by Eleanor Coerr. Visit the Math in Motion website at: www.mathinmotion.com

I ♥ Math in Motion

Sail ahead with Math in Motion

Curious George recycles his newspapers into a fleet of origami boats. Read *Curious George Rides a Bike* by H.A. Rey.

Color & Cut

Math Journals

A journal is a valuable tool in math class for students to express their ideas and reinforce classroom learning. The journal can provide a **"safe place"** for kids to write about their fears and concerns and enable the teacher to develop a more individual relationship with them.

Ask students to volunteer to read aloud from their journals to help start class discussions or to clarify points of confusion.

Through the math journal *self-assessment* and *reflection* are built into daily routines. Students can track their own work in progress and recount what they are learning, judging for themselves what is effective and what did not work.

See *Journal* diagram p. 51. The following suggestions are offered as a guideline from, *Writing to Learn Mathematics: Strategies that Work.*

1. **MAKE** an origami journal or purchase a spiral bound notebook. Write your name on it and decorate the outside.

2. **USE** the journal on a daily basis as part of a warm-up exercise or several days a week to suit your schedule.

3. **STORE** journals in the classroom on a permanent basis as it is easy for students to lose or misplace them.

4. **TO** motivate journal writing for the first time, engage the class in a process of self-discovery. **Ask students:**

   1) *How do I see myself as a math student?*
   2) *Write about past experiences with math.*
   3) *What are three strategies you can use to improve your study skills?*

5. **DON'T** limit how much they can write but encourage students to write a minimum of one paragraph for each assignment (at least three sentences).

6. **EACH** time students do class work, homework or a test they can use their journals to record both their progress and problems. *What were you working on today? How do you feel about this work? What problems did you encounter?*

7. **ENCOURAGE** students to leave space between entries in case they want to add information later and to give you room to respond.

8. **REMIND** students this is not a writing assignment and you are not judging their grammar or spelling.

9. **JOURNALS** only work if *you* respond to them. Ask students to draw a star next to the entry they want you to respond to and comment personally and positively to selected entries. Ask questions or make suggestions in response to student questions.

10. **MAKE** up a schedule you can manage on a weekly basis and select a few to reply to at a time. Collect A-M on Wednesday and N-Z the following week.

Pearls of Wisdom

A quotation paints a portrait of ideas and thoughts. The following are some of my favorite quotes. Write "Thought for the Week" on one side of the chalkboard and select an inspiring quotation, positive affirmation, word or symbol. Encourage students to bring in their favorite quotes, short poems or lyrics. At the end of the week, ask students to reflect on their thoughts in their origami journals (see *Journal* p. 51). Draw a picture to illustrate it. Ask students to share their responses with the class or another student.

Success comes in cans. Failure comes in can'ts. —Fred Seely

Are you part of the problem or part of the solution?

IF LIFE GIVES YOU A LEMON, MAKE LEMONADE.

PROBLEM SOLVING SUBTRACTS FROM DIFFICULTIES.

Minds are like parachutes — they function best when open.

You have to be a little patient if you're an artist, people don't always get you the first time. —Kate Millet

DON'T DISCOURAGE THE OTHER PERSON'S PLANS UNLESS YOU HAVE BETTER ONES TO OFFER.

DON'T SAY YOU DON'T HAVE ENOUGH TIME. YOU HAVE EXACTLY THE SAME NUMBER OF HOURS PER DAY THAT WERE GIVEN TO HELEN KELLER, PASTEUR, MICHELANGELO, MOTHER TERESA, LEONARDO DA VINCI, THOMAS JEFFERSON, AND ALBERT EINSTEIN. -*Life's Little Instruction Book*

THE IDEA IS TO WRITE IT SO THAT PEOPLE HEAR IT AND IT SLIDES THROUGH THE BRAIN AND GOES STRAIGHT TO THE HEART. —MAYA ANGELOU

None of us is as smart as all of us. -Japanese Proverb

An error is not a terror. -Haim Ginott

There are three kinds of people. . .those who make things happen, those who watch things happen, and those who wonder what happened.

ASK YOURSELF THESE QUESTIONS: WHO ARE YOU? WHAT KIND OF WORLD DO YOU WANT? -MUHAMMAD YUNUS, BANGLADESHI ECONOMIST, NOBEL PEACE PRIZE 2006

A winner never quits and a quitter never wins.

I'm a Japanese Fan

The fan is a symbol of good luck.
It represents the unfolding future.
Write something new that you have learned
about today inside each section of the fan.
Color the fan bright colors.

女　男　光　女　男　光

DOT TO DOT

Japan is famous for dancers who wear elaborate costumes.
This type of special entertainment has been popular for many years.
Connect the dots in order and color the dancer.

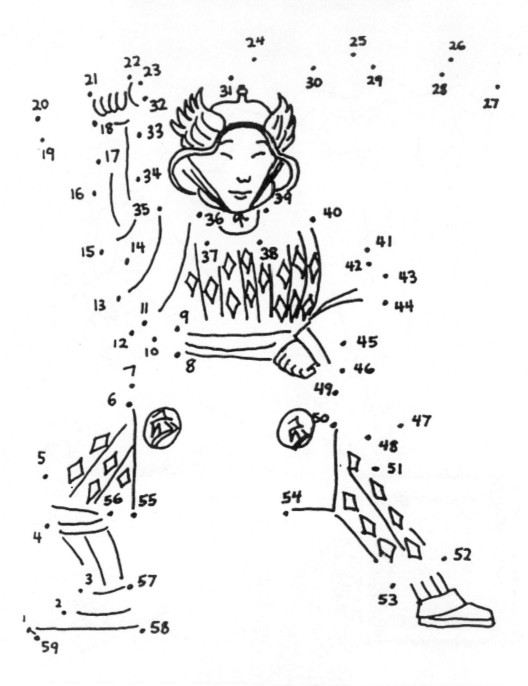

Maze Craze

Help the crane find the bonsai tree.
A bonsai is a Japanese miniature tree.
The crane is an international symbol of
peace, happiness and good luck.

Start

Finish

Bamboo is a woody perennial evergreen plant of the grass family that grows throughout Asia and other parts of the world. It can grow in many different climates from jungles to mountainsides. It varies in height from one foot (30 cm) to over 100 feet (30 m). In Japan, a bamboo forest sometimes surrounds a Shinto shrine as part of a sacred barrier. Bamboo is both decorative and useful for making a variety of objects from furniture, musical instruments, food, kitchen tools, floors, and construction. To learn more about bamboo, visit: www.americanbamboo.org.

Have Fun with Haiku

Haiku (hai-ku) is a Japanese poem about feelings and nature. It comes from two Japanese words meaning "play" and "poem." Each poem has three lines and contains 17 syllables. **The first and third lines have five syllables each and the second line has seven syllables.** Count the syllables in each line. These haiku poems were written by children.

The graceful crane soars
high above the mountain tops
teach me how to fly. --Erica

Flowers are blooming (5)
birds are singing in the trees (7)
spring is everywhere. (5)
    --Jason

Snow flakes in the sky
drift slowly to the wet ground
one cold winter day.
    --Seth

Close your eyes. Think about nature. Write a haiku and illustrate it.

FISH ARE FASCINATING ANIMALS

Kids for Saving Earth
the Pollution solution

Fish are amazing animals!

>=((('> Fish look so different from us--many people don't realize that they are intelligent, sensitive animals with their own unique personalities.

Check out these fun facts:

>=((('> Fish never close their eyes.

>=((('> Swordfish can swim more than 40 miles an hour.

>=((('> If a porcupine fish is confronted by danger, he or she will gulp water and inflate up to 2 feet, and sharp needles will pop out to frighten off predators.

Here are some things you can do to help your animal friends:

>=((('> Organize a clean-up day with your friends around local fishing spots. The number one cause of injuries and death to birds and other animals who live near the water is "fishing litter," like hooks, fishing lines, nets, and string. When animals come to the water for a drink, they get tangled and sometimes strangled in fishing litter. Head for a creek, lake, beach, or pond, and help out the animals by cleaning up.

>=((('> Create a "fish-friendly" display for your local library. Include pictures of different kinds of fish, useful facts and information.

>=((('> Fold a fish. Write a story or poem from the perspective of a fish. Tell how things may look from the fish's point of view. What things are important to the fish?

Cut out the diagram and make your own fish!

How to make the fish:

>=((('> a) Cut out the rectangle along dotted lines.
b) Fold corners 1, 2, and 3 forward
c) Fold corner 4 behind

• Alternative: Recycle old business cards or gift wrapping paper measuring 2" x 3.5"

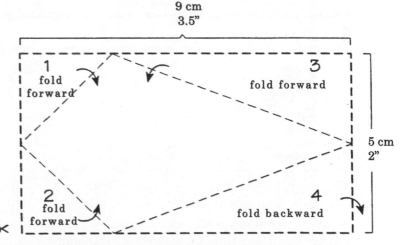

9 cm
3.5"

1
fold forward

3
fold forward

5 cm
2"

2
fold forward

4
fold backward

Resources: What are some ways we can create a more environmentally friendly and sustainable way of living? Read *50 Simple Things Kids Can Do To Save the Earth* by The Earth Works Group and *Making Kind Choices* by Ingrid Newkirk. Find out more amazing fun facts and activities from "Creating an Animal-Friendly World" at: www.teachkind.com

Can You Speak Japanese?

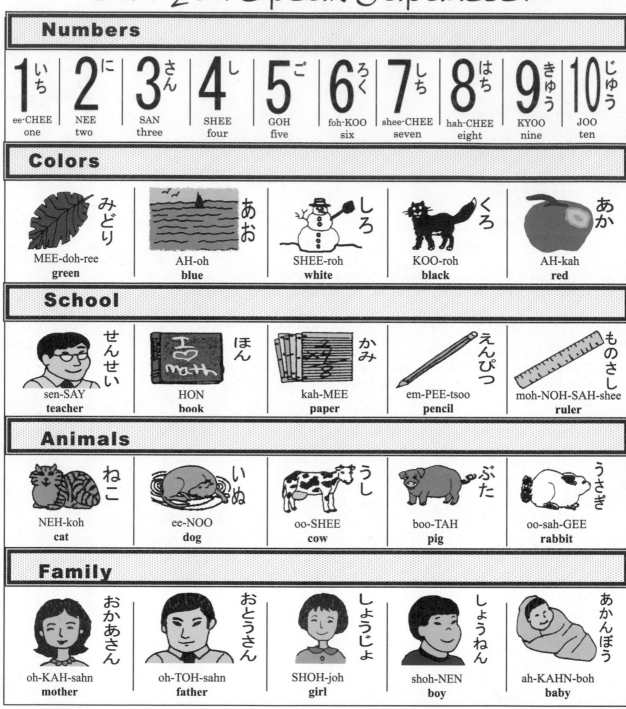

Numbers

1 いち	2 に	3 さん	4 し	5 ご	6 ろく	7 しち	8 はち	9 きゅう	10 じゅう
ee-CHEE	NEE	SAN	SHEE	GOH	foh-KOO	shee-CHEE	hah-CHEE	KYOO	JOO
one	two	three	four	five	six	seven	eight	nine	ten

Colors

みどり	あお	しろ	くろ	あか
MEE-doh-ree	AH-oh	SHEE-roh	KOO-roh	AH-kah
green	blue	white	black	red

School

せんせい	ほん	かみ	えんぴつ	ものさし
sen-SAY	HON	kah-MEE	em-PEE-tsoo	moh-NOH-SAH-shee
teacher	book	paper	pencil	ruler

Animals

ねこ	いぬ	うし	ぶた	うさぎ
NEH-koh	ee-NOO	oo-SHEE	boo-TAH	oo-sah-GEE
cat	dog	cow	pig	rabbit

Family

おかあさん	おとうさん	しょうじょ	しょうねん	あかんぼう
oh-KAH-sahn	oh-TOH-sahn	SHOH-joh	shoh-NEN	ah-KAHN-boh
mother	father	girl	boy	baby

The words on this page are written in Hiragana, a simple system of sounds used by Japanese children who are learning to read and write. By the time they finish high school they will learn over 2,000 characters.

Find the picture, how Japanese children might write the word, how it is pronounced in Japanese and the English word.

96

Writing Japanese Numbers

English	Japanese	Sound	Written
one	ichi	ee-chee	一
two	ni	nee	二
three	san	san	三
four	shi	shee	四
five	go	goh	五
six	roku	roh-koo	六
seven	shichi	shee-chee	七
eight	hachi	hah-chee	八
nine	ku	kyoo	九
ten	ju	joo	十
zero	zero	zee-row	〇
			七

Write your answers using Japanese words and numbers.

Example: 10 + 7 = 17   17 = ju + shichi = ju shichi

1. What is your age?_____

2. How many brothers and sisters do you have? _____

3. How many days are in a week? _____

4. Write your telephone number. _____

Tangram Puzzles

A Tangram is an ancient Chinese puzzle. The Chinese made tangram patterns to represent cats, boats and other objects.

The seven geometrical shapes:

one **square**

one **parallelogram**

two small **triangles**

one medium **triangle**

and two large **triangles**

fit together to make a **square.**

Label each shape and follow the directions.

1. Color the seven geometrical parts.
2. Cut out the shapes.
3. Make a square using all seven pieces.
4. Can you create these patterns?
5. Make your own designs.
6. Read *Grandfather Tang's Story*, teaching two-dimensional shapes through children's literature, (See Study Guide link, p. 115).

✂--

Optional: Duplicate on card stock.

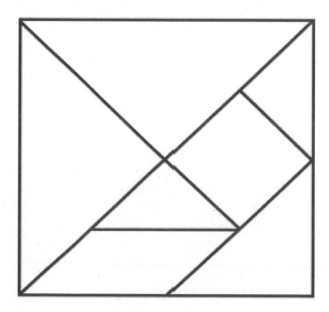

98

Fortune Cookies

Make up math fortunes to insert in the cookies. Have students make up their own math quotes or reinforce math vocabulary and concepts. To make fortunes, cut paper into strips about two inches long and ¾ inches wide. Type or write a fortune on each side. Ask a parent volunteer to make the cookies and insert the fortunes. Here are some examples of math quotes. Make up your own fortunes.

Count on MATH!　　　　Math is FUNctional.
I ♥ Math!　　　　　　Math makes a difference.
Math adds up.　　　　　It's the thought that counts.
Math Power for All.　　　Math teachers count a lot.

Recipe:　**1 cup margarine, softened (vegetable or soy)**
½ cup sugar
1 T of oil or soy yogurt
2 ½ teaspoons vanilla extract
3 ¼ cups flour
½ teaspoon baking powder

Suggestion: Test sugar alternatives like agave nectar to make sure they yield the same results. Try other healthy substitutes available at health food stores.

1. Mix together margarine, sugar and egg until smooth. Then add other ingredients. Mix everything together to form a ball of dough.

2. Lightly flour a wooden board or flat surface. With a rolling pin, roll half of the dough very thin. Use a circle-shaped cookie cutter or the top of a large glass about 2 ½ inches wide to cut circles in dough.

3. Put a fortune in each circle, off to one side. Fold the circle in half and then in half again. Pinch to close.

4. Preheat the oven to 425º.

5. Reroll cut scraps of dough and make cookies from them. Then roll and make cookies from the other half of the dough.

6. Bake cookies about 10 minutes or until they are lightly browned.

    Makes about 25 cookies.

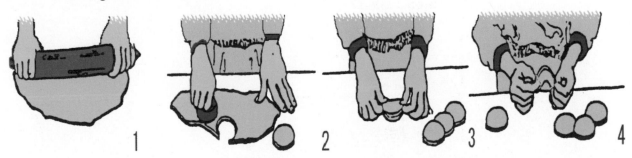

A Thousand Cranes of Origami

I will write 'peace' on your wings and you will fly all over the world.
--Sadako Sasaki, age 12

There is an old belief in Japan that a crane can live a thousand years; and that if you fold 1,000 paper cranes you will live a long life and they will keep you well. Twelve year old Sadako Sasaki made 644 paper cranes before she died of leukemia, ten years after the atomic bomb fell on Hiroshima. Friends and classmates collected 7,000,000 yen ($20,000) to build a monument dedicated to Sadako and other child victims of the bomb. Over the years, Sadako's life and death have become well known. The paper crane has become an international symbol of peace. Read *Sadako and the Thousand Paper Cranes* by Eleanor Coerr. Today, children from all over the world send paper cranes to decorate Sadako's monument, a statue of a young girl, standing atop a mountain, holding a golden crane in her outstretched arms. At the base of the statue, it reads:

> **This is our cry, this is our prayer: peace in the world.**

In 1999, *Wings for Peace, The World's Largest Paper Crane* was entered into the Guinness World Book of Records. Visit their website: http://www.sadako.org/largestcrane.htm. *Informed Democracy* offers videos based on the story at: www.sadako.com. *The Thousand Crane Club* invites children to participate in folding paper cranes to promote world peace. The crane is a challenging model and recommended for ages 8+. See library and Internet resources for instructions on folding cranes. Send cranes to:

Hiroshima International School
c/o 1000 Crane Club
3-49-1 Kurakake, Asakita-ku
Hiroshima, 739-1743 Japan
www.hiroshima-is.ac.jp/

How to Make an Origami Mobile

A mobile is a hanging ornament of parts that move. Origami makes a great mobile because it is lightweight and moves easily.

Materials: Several origami models, a needle, invisible thread, glue, thin soft wire and wire cutters. These items can be purchased in a craft or fabric store.

First, thread all your models. Vary the length of the thread to arrange the way you want each one to hang. (Fig. 1)

Cut a piece of wire and tie a model to each end. Make a loop at the end of the wire to keep the thread from slipping off. Glue the knots in place.

Tie a thread to the middle of the wire and slide it back and forth to balance the models. Glue the knot to the wire. (Fig. 2)

Tie the pair of models to one end of a longer wire. Place one model or another pair at the other end. Tie a thread to the wire and balance. (Fig. 3)

Continue to work from the bottom upward and use longer wires to hang all your models. Make the wires long enough so that none of the models touch each other as they move around in circles. Finally, balance a thread to hang up the mobile. An origami mobile of bright colors can decorate a classroom or make a colorful gift for a new baby or a special friend.

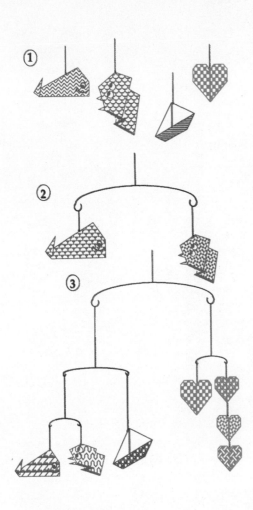

AaBbCcDdEeFfGgHhIiJjKkLlMmNnOoPpQqRrSsRrTtUuVvWwXxYyZz

MATHEMATICS

How many words can you find inside mathematics?
You can use the same letter more than once. Example: meet.
Write three sentences using as many of the words as you can.
Circle all the words you use in each sentence.

the
math
team

Number of Words:

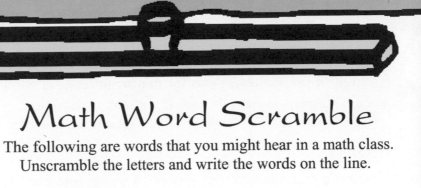

Math Word Scramble

The following are words that you might hear in a math class.
Unscramble the letters and write the words on the line.

1. mtgoyeer _____

2. strenitec _____

3. ymsetmry _____

4. gnale _____

5. qusera _____

6. ncogunter _____

7. cterglean _____

8. irgletna _____

9. arelpall _____

10. dupericpnerla _____

congruent

intersect   geometry

angle   symmetry   triangle

parallel   square   perpendicular

rectangle

Draw a Diagram

The national mathematics standards have identified the *appreciation* and *enjoyment* of mathematics as one of the national goals for mathematics education.

"...Mathematically powerful students think and communicate drawing mathematical ideas and using mathematical tools and techniques." - NCTM

Mathematical power has four dimensions: thinking, communication, ideas and techniques. Drawing a diagram challenges students to organize information, make connections, design, test, verify and reason. These activities support national goals for purposeful, enjoyable and active learning.

Directions: Peace of Paper

1 First examine and discuss diagrams and symbols that are used to create an origami model. Study sample diagrams from *Paper Folding Projects* (pp. 41-84) or models in other origami books.

2 Next ask students to practice drawing a diagram that represents a model they know how to fold. Include a key. Use symbols to diagram your model (see *Symbols*, p. 41). Draw other symbols as needed.

3 Then work in cooperative groups to design a solution or product that will bring world Peace. Students can draw their diagrams and ideas on a computer and use technology to enhance their project.

*Students exchange diagrams and fold their partner's model. Plan time for students to interpret, analyze, revise and edit their projects as needed. Encourage students to explain and justify their thinking. Students learn there can be *more* than one solution to the same problem. Assessment is in the PROOF!

*__Extension:__ Implement inquiry-centered curriculum. Asking questions and querying others' explanations is part of scientific inquiry. Scientific investigations sometimes result in new ideas for study or generate new methods of investigation. For more information, see National Science Resources Center-www.nsrconline.org.

Part VII

Resources

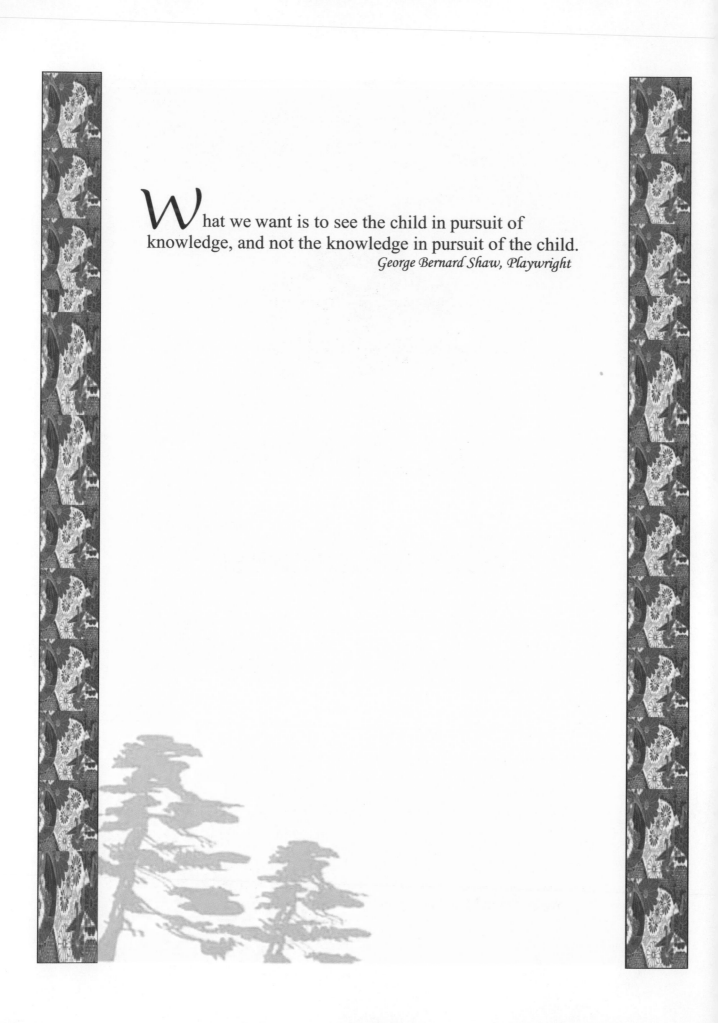

W hat we want is to see the child in pursuit of
knowledge, and not the knowledge in pursuit of the child.

George Bernard Shaw, Playwright

What to do with Origami

Origami offers *many* opportunities for educational and creative expression. Experiment with different paper materials, sizes and colors. Here are a few ideas. Can you think of more?

 Personalize notebooks; decorate greeting cards, stationery and packages.

 Make party decorations: invitations, cups, hats, place cards.

 Send a message of cheer to a friend; show you care.

 Prepare a presentation or book reprort with models.

 Make a friend—teach someone origami.

 Make scenes to illustrate a story or a lesson.

FRIENDS

 Decorate the holidays with origami; make ornaments for a tree, hearts for Valentine's Day, boats for Columbus Day, baskets for Easter, flowers for Spring, whales or other endangered animals for Earth Day.

 Pack a surprise model inside a lunch bag with a greeting.

 Make finger puppets. Create a play or dramatize a story.

 Build a fleet of boats, a village, farm animals or a diorama.

 Catch students doing something right and present them with a personalized model of a heart or sailboat.

 Create an Origami Learning Center in your classroom. Make an experience chart demonstrating the sequential steps of an origami model and invite students to fold it. Provide origami books, diagrams and paper supplies.

Children's Origami Exhibit

Origami USA

Origami by Children is an annual event. It is open to all children 18 years of age and younger. The Exhibit is available FREE to schools and libraries throughout the country. Request the Origami Exhibit for your school or local library. For more information contact Origami USA:

Origami by Children
15 West 77th Street
New York, New York 10024
☎ **(212) 769-5635**
www.origami-usa.org

Membership to Origami USA

Certificate of Merit

All Children Welcome

No Experience Required

Certificate of Achievement

is soaring ahead in
Mathematics

Teacher

Date

Glossary
English/Spanish
Inglés - Español

acute angle /ángulo agudo – an angle that has a measure less than 90°.

angle /ángulo – an angle is formed when two rays have a common endpoint.

answer /respuesta – the solution or response to a problem or a question.

area /área – the number of square units or surface inside a figure.

base /base – a side on which a geometrical figure stands.

base

bisect /bisecto – a line that divides a geometric figure into two congruent parts.

center /centro – the middle point, place or part.

column /columna – the tall, narrow portion of a figure or object.

congruent /congruente – line segments or figures with exactly the same size and shape.

count /contar – the total number or amount.

denominator /denominador – the bottom number in a fraction $\frac{3}{4}$
It tells the number of equal parts in the whole unit.

degree /grado – a unit for measuring angles and temperature. The symbol for degree is °.

diagonal /diagonal – a straight line that crosses in a slanting direction.

endpoint /punto final – a point where a line segment begins or ends.

equal /igual – the same in amount, size, number, or value. The symbol for equal is =.

even number /número par – divisible by two, a number that ends in 0, 2, 4, 6 or 8.

fraction /fracción – a number used to name parts of a whole or parts of a group.

geometry /geometría – a branch of mathematics that deals with the relationships between shapes, angles, lines and planes.

height /altura – a vertical distance usually upwards.

hexagon /hexágono – a polygon with six sides.

horizontal line /línea horizontal – a line parallel to or on level with the horizon.

intersection /intersección – to meet and cross.

intersecting lines /líneas que se cruzan – two or more lines that meet or cross at a common point.

isosceles triangle /triángulo isósceles – a triangle that has at least two congruent sides.

left /izquierda – to one side, opposite of right.

length /largo – the longest dimension of an object.

line /línea – a straight path that goes forever in both directions.

line of symmetry /línea de simetría – a line of folding so that the two halves of a figure match.

line segment /segmento de línea – a straight path that has two endpoints.

mathematics /matemáticas – the science of numbers, measurement and space.

measure /medir – to find the size or amount.

model /modelo – a design or representation.

numbers /nùmeros – symbols used for counting and measuring.

numerator /numerador – the top number in a fraction. $\frac{3}{4}$
It tells how many equal parts are being considered.

obtuse angle /ángulo obtuso – angles that measure greater than 90° and less than 180°.

octagon /octágono – a polygon with eight sides.

odd number /número impar – not divisible by two, numbers that end in 1, 3, 5, 7, 9.

opposite /contrario – as different in direction as can be.

parallel lines /líneas paralelas – lines in a plane that never intersect or meet.

parallelogram /líneas paralelogramo – a quadrilateral with 2 pairs of parallel lines.

pattern /modelo – an arrangement of forms, shapes and colors.

pentagon /pentágono – a polygon with five sides.

perpendicular lines /líneas perperndiculares – lines that intersect to form right angles.

plane /plano – a flat surface that continues infinitely in all directions.

point /punto – an exact location in space. (●)

polygon /polígono – a closed figure formed by three or more line segments.

quadrilateral /cuadrilateral – a polygon that has four sides.

ray /rayo – a portion of a line that extends forever in one direction only.

rectangle /rectángulo – a quadrilateral that has four right angles.

right /derecho – to one side, opposite of left.

| left | right |

right angle /ángulo recto – an angle that forms a square corner and measures 90º.

scalene triangle /triángulo escaleno – a triangle with all sides and angles different.

square /cuadrado – a rectangle with four sides of equal length.

trapezoid /trapezoide - a quadrilateral with one pair of parallel lines.

triangle /triángulo – a polygon with three sides; the sum of a triangle equals 180º.

vertex /vértice – the common endpoint of two rays that form an angle.

vertical line /línea vertical – straight up and down, for example a wall is vertical.

volume /volumen – the number of cubic units it takes to fit inside a solid figure.

width /anchura – a distance from side to side.

Numbers /Números

zero	0	cero		sixteen	16	dieciséis
one	1	uno		seventeen	17	diecisiete
two	2	dos		eighteen	18	dieciocho
three	3	tres		nineteen	19	diecinueve
four	4	cuatro		twenty	20	veinte
five	5	cinco		twenty-one	21	veintiuno
six	6	seis		thirty	30	treinta
seven	7	siete		thirty-one	31	treinta y uno
eight	8	ocho		forty	40	cuarenta
nine	9	nueve		forty-one	41	cuarenta y uno
ten	10	diez		fifty	50	cincuenta
eleven	11	once		sixty	60	sesenta
twelve	12	doce		seventy	70	setenta
thirteen	13	trece		eighty	80	ochenta
fourteen	14	catorce		ninety	90	noventa
fifteen	15	quince		hundred	100	cien

AMERICAN SIGN LANGUAGE 0-10

American Sign Language (ASL) is a complete, complex language that uses signs made with the hands and other movements, including facial expressions and body postures. It is the first language of many deaf North Americans, and one of several communication options available to deaf people. ASL is said to be the fourth most commonly used language in the United States. Children have the ability to sign even before they can speak. Studies show that this type of stimulation helps with language development and communication. Learn to sign with Koko the gorilla at: www.koko.org/world/signlanguage.html.

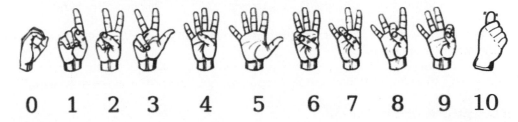

0 1 2 3 4 5 6 7 8 9 10

Suggested Readings & Resources

There are many origami books, videos and software from which to choose. Check your local library, bookstores and Internet resources. Add your favorites to the list.

National Organizations:

British Origami Society, 2a The Chestnuts, Countesthorpe, Leicester LE85TL, Great Britain, England. ☎0116-277-3870. www.britishorigami.org.uk.

National Clearinghouse for U.S.- Japan Studies, Indiana University, 2805 E. Tenth Street, Suite 120, Bloomington, Indiana 47408. ☎800-266-3815. www.indiana.edu/~japan (lesson plans, curriculum guides, activities).

National Council of Teachers of Mathematics. 1906 Association Drive, Reston, VA 22091. ☎800-235-7566. www.nctm.org (April is National Mathematics Education Month).

Origami USA. 15 West 77th Street, New York, NY 10024 ☎212-769-5635. (membership newsletter, annual convention, regional groups, books and supplies). www.origami-usa.org.

Books for Beginning Paper Folders:

Beech, R. (2001). *Origami Handbook*. London: Hermes House. (also published under the name, *Origami: The Complete Guide to the Art of Paper folding* – Intermediate-Advance level).

Kasahara, K. (1973). *Origami Made Easy*. Tokyo: Japan Publications. Easy - Intermediate.

Sakata, H. (1984). *Origami*. Tokyo: Harper & Row. Easy – Intermediate.

Smith. S. (2003). *Origami for the first time*. NY: Sterling. (color photos). Easy - Intermediate.

Videos and Software for Paper Folders:

Origami for Kids. Katsuhiko Takashige (2005) DVD, Learn to make frogs, cicadas, cranes, swans and more.

Origami: Square 1. Michael G. LaFosse (Instructional tapes and books). Origamido Studio. www.origamido.com

Sadako and the Thousand Paper Cranes (30 minutes) narrated by Liv Ullmann (1991) and *How to Fold a Paper Crane* by George Levenson (1994). Informed Democracy, P.O. Box 67, Santa Cruz, CA 95063. ☎800-827-0949. www.sadako.com. See *Send Cranes to Hiroshima* at: www.sadako.com/howtofold.html.

Paper Folding Stories:

Kallevig, C. P. (2001) *Fold Along Stories: Quick & Easy Origami Tales for Beginners*. Newburgh, Indiana: Storytime Ink International.

Kallevig, C. P. (1992) *Holiday Folding Stories: Storytelling and Origami Together for Holiday Fun*. Newburgh, Indiana: Storytime Ink International.

Pellowski, A. (1987) *Family Storytelling Handbook*. NY: Macmillian Publishing Company. (3 paper folding stories, "Something Special," "The Brothers Short/The Brothers Long," pp. 74-84, "Captain from Krakow," pp. 92-101).

Children's Literature: (multicultural)

Bang, M. (1985). *The Paper Crane.* NY: William Morrow & Company, Inc. (a mysterious man pays for his meal with a paper crane that comes alive, grades K-2).

Okawa, E. (1985) *The Adventures of the One Inch Boy.* Union City, CA: Heian International Inc. (a young boy triumphs despite his size, grades K-3).

Coerr, E. (1978) *Sadako and the Thousand Paper Cranes.* NY: G.P. Putnam's Sons. (a story about war, courage and peace, grades 3-6), video available.

Demi. (1990) *The Empty Pot.* NY: Henry Holt and Company. (Ping, a young Chinese boy discovers honesty is the best reward, grades K-2).

George, K. (2005). *Fold Me A Poem.* NY: Harcourt. (a collection of poems about origami animals, grades 2-5).

Juster, N. (1961) *The Phantom Tollbooth.* NY: Random House. (Milo and his friends travel to Digitopolis, grades 4-6), video available.

Kroll, V. (1994) *Pink Paper Swans.* Michigan: Wm. B. Eerdman. (a young African American girl and a Japanese woman find friendship through paper folding, grades 3-6).

Laurin, A. (1981) *Perfect Crane.* NY: Harper & Row. (a lonely magician gains friends through a paper crane he brings to life, grades 2-4).

Matsutani, M. (1968) *The Crane Maiden.* NY: Parents Magazine Press. (Japanese folktale, grades 3-5).

Pearl, B. (2005) *Whale of a Tale.* PA: Crane Books. (dive into reading with the adventures of a magic square, includes learning activities and how to fold a whale, great for early readers, grades PreK-2). Study Guide and Hand-outs: www.info@mathinmotion.com/studyguides

Rey, H. A. (1952) *Curious George Rides a Bike.* NY: Houghton. (George recycles his newspapers into an origami fleet of boats, instructions included, grades K-2).

Say, A. (1991) *Tree of Cranes.* NY: Houghton. (Holiday story, grades K-3).

Schroeder, A. (1994) *Lily and the Wooden Bowl.* NY: Delacote Press. (Japanese folktale, a young girl overcomes a variety of trials, grades 3-6).

Tompert, A. (1990) *Grandfather Tang's Story.* NY: Crown Publishers, Inc. (a tale told with tangrams, grades K-3). Study Guide: www.designedinstruction.com/prekorner/teaching-shapes-literature.html

Tsuchiya, Y. (1988) *The Faithful Elephants.* Boston: Houghton Mifflin Company. (a true story about animals, people and war, grades 3-5).

Math Resources:

Arem, C. (1993). *Conquering Math Anxiety: A Self-Help Workbook.* CA: Brooks/Cole.

Bendick, J. (1989). *Mathematics Illustrated Dictionary.* NY: Franklin Watts.

Cipoletti, B., Wilson, N. (2004, August). Turning Origami into the Language of Mathematics. *Mathematics Teaching in the Middle School,* NCTM, Volume 10, Issue 1, p. 26.

Countryman, J. (1992). *Writing to Learn Mathematics: Strategies that Work.* NH: Heinemann.

Day, L., Langbort, C. & Skolnick, J. (1986). *How to Encourage Girls in Math and Science.* Palo Alto, CA: Dale Seymour Publisher.

Engel, P. (1988, June). Origami: The Mathematician's Art. *Discover,* pp. 54-61.

Higginson, W. & Colgan, L. (2001, August). Algebraic Thinking through Origami. *Mathematics Teaching in the Middle School,* NCTM, Focus Issue 2004-2005, Volume 6, Issue 6, p. 343.

Kaplan, A., Keating, E. & Boretz, C. (1991, March). *Careers for Number Lovers.* CT: Millbrook Press.

Masunaga, D. (2002, January). Origami: It's Not Just For Squares. *Student Math Notes,* NCTM.

National Council of Teachers of Mathematics (NCTM) (2000). *Principles and Standards for School Mathematics.*

NCTM. *Curriculum and Evaluation Standards for School Mathematics.* (1989). Reston, VA: Author.

NCTM. Olson, A. T. (1991). *Mathematics through Paper Folding. (Junior High).*

National Research Council. *Everybody Counts: A Report to the Nation on the Future of Mathematics Education* (1989). Washington DC: National Academy Press.

Paulos, J. (1988). *Innumeracy—Mathematical Illiteracy and Its Consequences.* NY: Hill and Wang.

Phibbs, M. (1991, October). *Lessons in Listening and Learning. The Science Teacher.* 58(7), pp. 40-43.

Sinicrope, R. & Mick, H. W. (1992, October). *Multiplication of Fractions through Paper Folding, Arithmetic Teacher,* pp. 116-121.

Sze, S. (2005, March). An Analysis of Constructivism and the Ancient Art of Origami. Niagara University, Innovations in Inclusive School Development, Conference Proceedings.

Winter, S. S. & Caruso, J. (1993). *Spanish Math Terms, Palabras fundamentales de matemáticas.* Portland, Maine: J. Weston Walch.

Supplies & Other Resources

50 Simple Things Kids Can Do to Save the Earth. Andrews and McMeel (1990). The Earth Works Group, NY: Universal Press Syndicate Company.

A Whack on the Side of the Head: How You Can Be More Creative. Roger von Oech (1983). NY: Warner Books. www.creativethink.com.

Animal Crusaders. 965 Alamo Drive, Suite 306, Vacaville, CA 95687. ☎707-451-1306. email for a FREE teacher subscription at: info@fund.org. website: www.fund.org.

Social Learning Theory. Albert Bandura. (1977). NY: General Learning Press.

Children's Peace Project. P.O. Box 9509, Santa Fe, New Mexico 87504. ☎505-989-4482. Influenced by the children's peace statue in Japan, American children built this as a sign of their "Hope for a Peaceful Future." www.networkearth.org/world/peace.html.

Educators for Social Responsibility. 23 Garden Street, Cambridge, MA 02138. ☎617-492-1764. (conflict resolution, environmental awareness, meetings) www.esrnational.org.

Multiple Intelligences: The Theory in Practice. Howard Gardner. (1993). NY: Basic Books.

Haiku, One Breath Poetry. Naomi Wakan. (1993). Canada: Pacific-Rim Publishers.

Making Kind Choices: Everyday Ways to Enhance Your Life Through Earth and Animal-Friendly Living. Ingrid Newkirk. (2004). NY: St. Martin's Griffin.

Peace Pole Makers USA. 7221 S. Wheeler Road, Maple City, MI 49664. ☎231-334-4567. www.peacepoles.com. Peace poles stand 6 feet tall and carry a universal message, "May peace prevail on Earth" in a variety of languages. Organize a fundraiser to purchase a peace pole for your school or organization to promote world peace.

Teaching Tolerance Magazine. 400 Washington Avenue, Montgomery, AL 36104. ☎334-264-0286. www.splcenter.org. (free resources, videos, posters and materials for educators).

The Global Link Newsletter. The World Peace Prayer Society, 26 Benton Road, Wassaic, NY 12592. ☎800-732-2354. www.worldpeace.org/glinknews.html. (sponsors the Peace Pole Project, Peace Pals and other peace related activities).

The Joyful Child. Peggy Jenkins. (1989). Arizona: Harbinger House. www.joy4u.org.

The Power and Promise of Humane Education. Zoe Weil. (2004). Canada: New Society Publishers. www.humaneeducation.org.

Women's History Catalog. 343 Industrial Drive, Suite 4, Santa Rosa, CA 95403. ☎707-636-2888. www.nwhp.org. *Outstanding Women in Mathematics and Science.*

Notes

None of us is as SMART as all of us.
-Japanese Proverb

It's a special world full of special children and everyone is special in their own way

SHOOT FOR THE MOON even if you miss, you'll still land among the stars.
-Les Brown

An error is not a terror. -Haim Ginott

☑ Read: *Between Parent and Child* and *Between Teacher and Child* by Haim Ginott

Barbara Pearl

Winner of the
"Ezra Jack Keats" Award

Barbara Pearl is an international award winning educator and author. She has an M.A. in Education from La Salle University where she received the 2003 Graduate Faculty Award for Excellence in Academic Achievement and Leadership. She also attended schools in England and France. Barbara developed *Math in Motion* in 1979 while working as a classroom teacher. Her background in elementary education and mathematics inspired her to explore strategies that get students and teachers excited about mathematics and learning.

A featured speaker on National TV and in *Creative Classroom*, Ms. Pearl is the three-time recipient of the National Library Week Award including the "Ezra Jack Keats" Award for her multicultural programs. Ms. Pearl participated in the John F. Kennedy Center for the Performing Arts, "Artists as Educators" Seminar. She presents professional staff development and student workshops helping schools and districts improve the quality of mathematics and literacy instruction. As an international speaker, Barbara has traveled extensively throughout the United States, Europe and Asia, including China, Japan, and Russia.

Ms. Pearl installed the first "Origami & Math" Exhibit at The Franklin Institute Science Museum, the Free Library of Philadelphia and the Philadelphia International Airport. Her book has been translated into Spanish, *Matemàticas en Movimiento*. She wrote her first children's book, *Whale of a Tale*, integrating origami and storytelling for early readers. A percentage of sales is donated to humanitarian organizations that support global education.

"I will write 'peace' on your
wings and you will fly
all over the world."
-Sadako Sasaki, age 12

♥**Dear Friends**--Thank you for your commitment and dedication to creative approaches to teaching and learning mathematics. My vision is that *Math in Motion* will be a part of every child's educational experience. In Japan, children learn origami at home and in kindergarten. Today, many schools in the West integrate origami in the classroom. There is something very special about transforming a piece of paper into a work of art that nurtures a child's mind as well as their spirit. Research has shown that paper folding, particularly in the elementary school years, is a unique and valuable addition to the curriculum (Sze, 2005). Origami is not only fun, but also an innovative method for developing critical skills. I have received letters from all over the world – from kids who have failed in mathematics and then succeeded, teachers and parents apprehensive about teaching math for the very first time, PTAs/PTOs, gifted and ELL students, private and public schools, students working on master's degrees and doctorates, education and resource specialists, consultants, retired teachers, librarians, museum directors, publishers who have integrated origami into their textbooks, Scouts, homeschools, schools for the deaf, and teachers who work with juveniles in detention centers – all sharing their heartfelt experiences. Many of the letters are posted on the Math in Motion website on the "Comments" page and may be featured in Book II. People often ask how they can bring a workshop to their area. For more information, please call or visit our website. I hope you will continue to write and share how origami has touched your life too.

Math in Motion
668 Stony Hill Road, #233
Yardley, PA 19067
info@mathinmotion.com
www.mathinmotion.com
☎ **(215) 321-5556**

Math in Motion

Where Every Child Counts!
15ᵗʰ Anniversary

Math in Motion: Origami in the Classroom K-8

Easy to follow, step-by-step instructions develop basic educational skills. The color illustrations, interdisciplinary lessons and teacher scripts support National Mathematics Standards, cultural diversity and cooperative learning activities to create FUN for kids of *all* ages. English/Spanish Glossary, 120 pages (Spanish edition available).
ISBN-13: 978-0-9647924-3-2

Math in Motion..........................**$24.95**

Quantity Discounts Available!

Visit website oval.

Visit our website:
mathinmotion.com

"...nicely written, well-organized and deserves to be in classrooms everywhere!"
- -George William Bratton III, Managing Editor, Ideal School Supply

MIM Resource Kit

The complete package! Includes the *Math in Motion* book (hole punched), in an attractive bright yellow silk screened binder, two inside pockets, a teacher pack of origami paper (50 sheets) and a surprise gift!

Designed to hold lesson plans, hand-outs and other related resources; conveniently organizes all your materials for easy reference and use! Dimensions 10" x 12" x 1"

MIM Resource Kit......... **$39.95**
(Spanish Edition Available, Matemáticas en Movimiento: Origami en el Salón de Clases)

Peace Cranes

A beautiful origami crane folded from hand-made washi Japanese paper. Each crane is strung with an Australian lead crystal heart. An assortment of colors and patterns. Request a color or let us choose. Great for the classroom, display or give as a gift.
Peace Crane.....1/$9.95 or 2/$17.95

Math & Literacy Workshops K-8
"Finally, a workshop where I could do more than just listen!"

✓ Staff Development
✓ Student Workshops
✓ Family Math Night

Hands-on ● Practical ● Interactive

Unfold a positive attitude towards learning! Discover new classroom-tested techniques and proven strategies for using best practices to develop research and standards-based concepts and skills for teaching *reading, writing and mathematics*. Half-day, 1, 2, and 3 day workshops are custom tailored to meet YOUR exact needs. You will be in a hurry to get back to your classroom to try these ideas out for yourself! For more information, contact Math in Motion at:

info@mathinmotion.com
www.mathinmotion.com
☎ **(215) 321-5556**

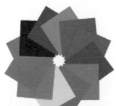

Whale of a Tale PreK-2
Storytelling & Origami
n the adventures of a magic
are that transforms into
ferent origami shapes.
ludes beautiful watercolor
strations, features how to fold
hale and learning activities.
rdcover, 32 pages
3N-13: 978-0-9647924-7-0
hale of a Tale............$14.95

GIANT Classroom
Origami Paper Packs
pecial giant **assortment** of **SOLID**
-inch squares in festive colors or **FOIL**
rigami paper in gold or silver. Perfect
or projects in *Math in Motion* books.
Assortment Pack (400 sheets)...$24.95
Foil Paper (500 sheets)...........$34.95

♥A percentage of sales is donated to humanitarian organizations that support global education.

MATH IN MOTION ORDER FORM
668 Stony Hill Road, #233, Yardley, PA 19067 ☎(215) 321-5556
FAX: (215) 310-9412 ➤ info@mathinmotion.com ➤ www.mathinmotion.com

Ship to: Please type or print clearly

☐ Ms. ☐ Mrs. ☐ Mr. ☐ Dr.

Name_____

School _____ District _____

Street Address _____

City/State/Zip _____

Day Phone_____ Eve Phone _____

Email Address _____ Position/Grade_____

☐ Please contact me about wor

Resource Materials:

Item					ount
Math in Motion Book (English					
Math in Motion Book (Spanis					
MIM Resource Kit (English					
(Kit includes Math in Motion book, 3- teacher pack of origami paper and a					
MIM Resource Kit (Spanish					
Whale of a Tale (English Edit					
Giant Assortment Paper Pac					
Foil Paper, Circle: Gold or S					
Peace Cranes					

Method of Payment:

Please make payable to: M .mathinmotion.com

☐ Check ☐ Money Orde er ☐ Amer. Exp.

Card # _____ onth/_____year

Card Verification Number: (l

Mailing Address on credit car

Authorized Signature: (as it app

Shipping & Handling:

Orders up to $25.00, add $5
Each additional $25.00, add
Quantity, Rush and Interna
Orders, please email or call.
info@mathinmotion.com
☎(215) 321-5556

TOTAL AMOUNT

DATE DUE

Thank you for your order!